KYTICE

THE AMBER POETS

Karel Jaromír Erben
Kytice

Translated from the Czech by
Susan Reynolds

The Amber Poets
Series Editor
Michael Tate

JANTAR PUBLISHING
London 2025

THE AMBER POETS
Book 2

Kytice
Karel Jaromír Erben

First published in London, Great Britain, in 2024 by
Jantar Publishing Ltd
www.jantarpublishing.com

First published in Prague in 1853 as *Kytice*
This version is taken from the expanded 1861 edition and the 1948 Melantrich edition
Second edition published on 21 November 2020
to commemorate the 150th anniversary of the poet's death
This third edition published in 2025 as Amber Poets volume 2

Translation © 2020 Susan Reynolds
Introduction © 2020 Geoffrey Chew
Cover and book design © Davor Pukljak 2025

The right of Susan Reynolds to be identified as translator of this work
has been asserted in accordance with the Copyright, Design and Patents Act 1988.

No part of this book may be reproduced or utilised in any form or by any means,
electronic or mechanical, including photocopying, recording, or by any information
storage and retrieval system, without written permission.

A CIP record of this book is available from the British Library
ISBN 978-1-914990-28-1

Contents

Introduction . . . . *I*

KYTICE
a book of poetry by Karel Jaromír Erben

The Posy	1
The Treasure	3
The Wedding Shirts	23
The Noonday Witch	35
The Golden Spinning-wheel	37
Christmas Eve	51
The Wild Dove	59
Záhoř's Bed	65
The Water-goblin	85
The Willow Tree	97
The Lily	103
The Daughter's Curse	107
The Prophetess	111

More Information on The Amber Poets Series *121*

Introduction

Karel Jaromír Erben's *Kytice* ('A Garland', 'A Bouquet', or 'A Posy'), the present collection of original ballads reworking Czech folk themes, first published in 1853,[1] is one of the best-loved canonical texts of 19th-century Cze ch literature, together with Karel Hynek Mácha's epic poem, *May* [*Máj*] (1836), and Božena Němcová's novel of rural life, *The Grandmother* [*Babička*] (1855).

Erben, one of twin boys, sons of a shoemaker, was born in the town of Miletin near Jitschin [Miletín u Jičína] on 7 November 1811, and died in Prague on 21 November 1870. He received his elementary education (including instruction in music) at a school where his grandfather and uncle were teachers, and proceeded from there to *Gymnasium* at Königgrätz [Hradec Králové] (1825–31), supporting himself by giving music lessons. (A little later he was reproached for making his piano-playing a substitute for real-life experience.[2]) At Prague University he studied arts and law (1831–3), and encountered outstanding members of the younger generation of those writing in Czech, including K. H. Mácha and the dramatist Josef Kajetán Tyl, as well as some of those writing in German.

---

1 Karel Jaromír Erben, *Kytice z pověstí národních* [*A Bouquet of National Legends*] (Prague: Jaroslav Pospíšil, 1853); 2nd edition, K. J. Erben, *Kytice z básní* [*A Bouquet of Poems*] (Prague: Jaroslav Pospíšil, 1861).
2 Šebestián Hněvkovský, letter to the 25-year-old Erben: 'Ich muß es Euch geradezu sagen, daß Ihr nicht zweimal einen Geliebten vorstellen kennet; denn Ihr sitzt und wieder sitzt und spielt Forte-Piano, ohne das verliebte Mädchen durch einen verliebten Blick, Händedruck oder süssen Kuß etc. von der Gegenliebe zu überzeugen', quoted in Jakobson, 'Poznámky k dílu Erbenovu: I.' (as in n. 21 below), at p. 159.

Erben's vocation was in the first place as an archivist, antiquarian and folklorist, rather than as a poet. He became an assistant to the historian František Palacký, famous 'father of the nation', assembling material from provincial and rural archives in Bohemia, and this work made it possible for him to work as an active ethnologist, collecting Czech folk-songs, which he began to publish from 1841,[3] and Czech and other Slavonic folk legends, along lines established by the brothers Grimm, which he published from 1844.[4] In 1848, the year of revolutions, he was involved in the abortive Prague Slavic Congress [*Slovanský sjezd*] of which Palacký was president; subsequently, like Palacký, he retreated from active political engagement. From the 1850s Erben was employed as an archivist in Prague. Working at the National Museum, he edited numerous older Czech texts, including the complete writings in Czech of the reformer Jan

---

3 Karel Jaromír Erben, *Písně národní v Čechách* [*Folk-Songs in Bohemia*] (Prague: Jan Host. Popíšil, 3 volumes, 1841–5). Erben enlisted the help of the composer and cleric Jan Pavel Martinovský (1808–73) to provide piano accompaniments to the melodies, and these were published as *Nápěvy písní národních v Čechách: Sbírka K. Jaromíra Erbena* [*Melodies of Folk-Songs in Bohemia: The Collection of K. J. Erben*] (Prague: J. Hoffmann, 5 volumes, 1842–70). A second enlarged edition of the folk-songs was published as *Prostonárodní české písně a říkadla s přílohou nápěvů* [*Bohemian Folk-Songs and Riddles, with an Annex of Melodies*] (Prague: Jaroslav Pospíšil, 1862; modern edition, as *Prostonárodní české písně a říkadla: s nápěvy do textu vřaděnými*, ed. Zdeněk Mišurec (Prague: Panton, vydavatelství Českého hudebního fondu, 6 volumes, 1985–90).

4 Erben's editions of folk legends include his *Sto prostonárodních pohádek a pověstí slovanských v nářečích původních: čítanka slovanská s vysvětlením slov* [*100 Slavonic Fairy-Tales and Folk Legends in the Original Dialects: A Slavonic Reader with Glossary*] (Prague: Kober, 1865, in English translation as *Panslavonic Folklore in Four Books: Translated from Karel Jaromir Erben's 'A Hundred Genuine Popular Slavonic Fairy Stories' in the Original Dialects and Compared with Notes, Comments, Tables, Illustrations and Supplementary Essays*, trans. Walter W. Strickland, New York: B. Westermann Co., 1930); and his *Vybrané báje a pověsti národní jiných větví slovanských* [*Selected Folk Tales and Legends from Other Slavonic Branches*] (Prague: Spolek pro vydávání laciných knih českých, 1869; modern edition, Prague: Městská knihovna v Praze, 2011).

Hus, wrote entries, principally on mythology, for the first Czech encyclopedia (the so-called *Riegrův slovník naučný*, published from 1860), and translated texts from other Slavonic languages.

Kytice and the Literary Ballad in Bohemia

In *Kytice*, Erben reworked some of the Czech legends he had assembled into a collection of literary ballads, serious in tone, with brief notes giving details of their sources in national legend and of some of their parallels in the folklore of other nations.[5]

His collection owes something to the celebrated collection of folk and other poetry by Thomas Percy (1765), well-known in continental Europe. This had helped to establish the notion that folk ballads and folk-songs represent a natural literature equal or superior in status to learned prose and poetry, and provided material for Erben, either directly or at second hand.[6]

Closer to Erben than Percy, however, lies Johann Gottfried Herder, in his *Volkslieder* (1778-9).[7] Although Herder's

---

5 The general literature on Erben and *Kytice* is very extensive, especially in Czech. The older standard monograph is Julius Dolanský, Karel Jaromír Erben, *Odkazy pokrokových osobností naší minulosti* (Prague: Melantrich, 1970), and a more recent anniversary volume is Zuzana Urválková and Alena Pospíšilová, eds., *Kytice u nás: sborník ke 150. výročí prvního vydání básnické sbírky Karla Jaromíra Erbena* (Jilemnice: Vydavatelství Gentiana pro Městskou knihovnu Jičín, 2003). Useful brief introductions for English-speaking readers can be found in Robert B. Pynsent, 'Erben, Karel Jaromír', *The Everyman Companion to East European Literature*, ed. Robert B. Pynsent and S. I. Kanikova (London: Dent, 1993), p. 104, and James Naughton, 'Czech and Slovak Nationalism', in *Encyclopedia of the Romantic Era, 1760-1850* (London: Routledge, 2003).
6 Thomas Percy, *Reliques of Ancient English Poetry: Consisting of Old Heroic Ballads, Songs, and Other Pieces of our Earlier Poets, Chiefly of the Lyric Kind, Together with Some Few of Later Date* (London: J. Dodsley, 1765).
7 Johann Gottfried Herder, *Volkslieder, nebst untermischten andern Stücken*, 2 vols. (Leipzig: Weygand, 1778-9); new edition as Johann von Müller, ed., *Stimmen der Völker in Liedern*, Johann Gottfried von Herder's sämmtliche Werke, pt. 8 (Tübingen: Cotta, 1807).

collection includes more than 20 translations from Percy's, it has been persuasively argued by Matias Martinez that Herder's notion of folk-song was different from Percy's. Herder's central interest is in the 'lyric' quality his texts possess, and he did not provide historical references for his texts to establish their meaning for modern readers, as Percy did. For him, rather, a 'language of sentiment' [*Sprache der Empfindung*] is the essence of poetry, particularly of *Naturpoesie* as found in folk-song, and this depends on the 'tone' [*Ton*] or 'melody' [*Weise*] of that language. This 'tone' is not merely an indication that *Naturpoesie* is close to music; it also establishes a rapport between folk poet and folk audience, through poetry whose subjects are 'anthropological stock situations taken from the repertoire of a community's traditional culture', held in common by a poet and his audience.[8] Even a modern reader should therefore be capable of entering into the experience of the original folk audience. But such poetry is not necessarily ancient: a modern poet may also emulate folk lyric successfully. So, besides *Naturpoesie* as embodied in folk-song, Herder includes *Kunstpoesie* by modern poets such as Goethe who echo its 'tone', and it is this 'tone' that marks Erben's literary ballads.

Other *Kunstballaden* had also preceded those in *Kytice*. Czech translations had already been made of some ballads by Johann Wilhelm Ludwig Gleim (1719–1803). And the ballad 'Lenore', by Gottfried August Bürger (1747–94), published in 1774, and sensationally popular throughout Europe, was very well-known in Bohemia. Its fashionable turn towards

---

8 Matias Martinez, 'Lyric – Keeper of the Past: On the Poetics of Popular Poetry in T. Percy's *Reliques of Ancient Poetry* and J.G. Herder's *Volkslieder*', in *Genres as Repositories of Cultural Memory*, ed. Hendrik van Gorp and Ulla Musarra-Schroeder, Textxet: Studies in Comparative Literature, vol. 29 (Amsterdam and Athens, GA: Rodopi, 2000), pp. 205–17, quoted here *passim* from pp. 211–13.

the Gothic and the terrifying supernatural is also evident in *Kytice*, and it provides an obvious model for the fearful nocturnal journey in Erben's 'The Wedding Shirts', as also for that in Goethe's well-known 'Erlkönig' of 1782. Set to music, 'Lenore' became the first great success of Václav Jan Tomášek (1774–1850), the principal Prague composer of the period, in 1806,[9] and it was also translated into Czech by Josef Jungmann (1773–1847). Unlike Herder's ballads, it has a historical setting, and this connects it with Bohemia. The young Lenore blasphemously blames God for the failure of Wilhelm, her betrothed, to return from serving in the Prussian army at the Battle of Prague (1757); but Wilhelm returns mysteriously at night from Bohemia, and carries her back with him on a terrifying journey of hundreds of miles, perhaps as punishment for the blasphemy, to the longed-for marriage bed, which is revealed as his own grave.[10] And the motif of the threatening supernatural recurs in the well-known Czech ballad, 'Toman and the Wood Nymph' [*Toman a lesní panna*] by František Ladislav Čelakovský (1799–1852), in his *Ohlas písní českých* [*Echo of Czech Songs*] of 1839, in which Čelakovský seeks a poetic style that is distinctively national and in contrast to his *Ohlas písní ruských* [*Echo of Russian Songs*] of 1829.[11]

Erben had worked intensively in 1851 and 1852 on the first edition of *Kytice* (1853), which contained twelve poems,

---

[9] Václav Tomášek [Wenzel Tomaschek], who (unlike Franz Schubert) gained Goethe's approval for his setting of 'Erlkönig', secured a permanent position as composer-in-residence to Count Bucquoy on the strength of his 'Lenore'.
[10] Erben's debt to Bürger was long ago recognized: see Miloslav Hýsek, 'Bürgerovy ohlasy v české literatuře' ['Echoes of Bürger in Czech literature'], *Listy filologické*, year 35, no. 2 (1908), pp. 106–21.
[11] František Ladislav Čelakovský, *Ohlas písní českých* [*Echo of Czech Songs*] (Prague: Umělecká beseda, 1839).

some newly composed, including the introductory poem that shares the name of the collection, '*Kytice*' (here translated as 'The Posy'), and several that had been written or published previously: 'The Treasure' ['*Poklad*'], published in 1838, 'The Wedding Shirts' ['*Svatební košile*'], 'The Golden Spinning-wheel' ['*Zlatý kolovrat*'], and 'Christmas Eve' ['*Štědrý den*'], published in 1848. And 'Záhoř's Bed' ['*Záhořovo lože*'] exists in an earlier version from 1836. Another poem, 'The Lily' ['*Lilie*'], was added for the second edition of 1861. The poems are by no means uniform, and seem to have been grouped by Erben, with distinctive prosodic structures, arguably exhibiting differences and similarities of genre. So the introductory poem, 'The Posy', and the final poem, 'The Prophetess: Fragments' ['*Věstkyně: Úlomky*'], are a matching patriotic pair, and both are cast in quatrains of alternating eleven-syllable and eight-syllable verses, with ABAB rhyme-schemes. The first poem deals with the loss of the motherland, in ages long ago, discovered on a grave-mound; the final one presents a prophecy of her rediscovery and rebirth, invoking the legendary prophetess Libuše, fictively presented, as the first one was, as a chance, fragmentary discovery. 'The Treasure' and 'The Wedding Shirts' are also a pair: both are narrative ballads, with eight-syllable verses, in stanzas of varying length, but trochaic and iambic respectively, differing evidently for the sake of the action, and with varied rhyme-schemes. (Another, more artificial, version of the same pattern, adding verses of three and seven syllables for the sake of the short repeated interpolations, is employed for 'The Daughter's Curse' ['*Dceřina kletba*'].) And, as Xavier Galmiche points out, the 'water-goblin' ['*Vodník*'] in the poem of that name in fact 'resorts successively to four different types of verse [...] in the search for prosody fine enough to adapt to the nuances of a changing expression'.[12] 'Christmas Eve' is even more varied, no doubt for the same reason.

The poem 'Záhoř's Bed' occupies a special position in the collection. It is more irregular in prosody than the other poems, more indebted to Baroque imagery, and sometimes regarded as an orthodox Catholic counterblast to the irreligion of Mácha's poem *May* [*Máj*], with which it shares the image of the young, disconsolate 'pilgrim'. Erben himself suggests that the legend, existing also in Polish and Lusatian variants, dates from the earliest introduction of Christianity to the Slavonic world.[13] Its plot, like that of the legends on which it is based, is not unified. The young man introduced at the outset has a mission to avoid damnation by entering hell and cancelling the pact his father once made with the Devil; though he succeeds in this, this theme seems less important to the poem than another, which is his mission to bring the ogre Záhoř, a 'green man' [*muž lesní*] he meets on the way, to repentance, and the title of the poem indicates that it is the lurid tortures that the young man finds in hell, awaiting Záhoř, that are of principal interest. (One of these, the 'iron maiden', a cabinet in the shape of a human being, with internal spikes, used according to Erben's explanatory notes for executing aristocrats

---

12 Xavier Galmiche, 'Postface, *Un bouquet* de Karel Jaromír Erben: L'originalité difficile', in Daniel Larangé and others, trans., *Kytice, un bouquet de légendes tchèques: édition bilingue* (Paris: Editions Persée, 2001), pp. 202–15, here quoted at p. 208 n. 11: '[Erben] semble multiplier les solutions prosodiques – ainsi *Le Génie du lac* recourt-il successivement à quatres types de vers différents – animé d'une avidité pour ainsi dire expérimentale dans la recherche d'une métrique assez fine pour s'adapter aux nuances d'une expression changeante'.

13 The Lower Lusatian version, 'Lipskulijanowe łože', in which Záhoř is called 'Lipskulijan', had been published in the original and in German translation in Leopóld Haupt and Jan Ernst Smoleŕ [Johann Ernst Schmaler], eds., *Prόznicki Serskego ludu we gόrejcnych a dołojcnych Łužyach, ludoj z ust napisane / Volkslieder der Wenden in der Ober- und Nieder-Lausitz, aus Volksmunde aufgezeichnet*, pt. 2 (Gryme [Grimma]: J.M. Gebhardt, 1843), pp. 176–8. Palacký was one of the subscribers to the edition.

in preference to decapitation, and said by him to have existed 'in the White Tower in Prague', is now thought never to have existed before its invention in literature in the early 19th century.[14])

The legitimacy of Erben's Czech prosody in his verse was widely debated in the 19th century. It relies in part on distinctions between long and short syllables on the model of Greek and Latin verse (*časomíra*, 'measurement of time'), rather than on distinctions between stressed and unstressed syllables, though in due course the latter came to seem more 'natural' for Czech poetry, in terms of its relation to the language, both as spoken and as set to music.[15] It is unsurprising, then, that though composers were not slow in responding to Erben's poetry, as indicated below, the complexity of his prosody in *Kytice* may have discouraged some of them from setting any of it directly to music. Even a composer as central to the Revival as Bedřich Smetana set no verse by Erben, preferring the simpler, more anodyne verse of Vítězslav Hálek's *Songs of Evening* [*Večerní písně*]. Moreover, the bloodthirstiness of some of the Kytice poems was also an unwelcome feature to some composers, once the Gothic had become less fashionable.

Kytice and Gender

Erben's title for the collection, 'Kytice', also used for the title of the first poem in the collection, has often been repeated in later Czech collections of poetry and music. It immediately raises the question of gendering. The metaphor of a collection of flowers,

---

14 See Wolfgang Schild, *Die Eiserne Jungfrau: Dichtung und Wahrheit* (Rothenburg ob der Tauber: Mittelalterliches Kriminalmuseum, 1998).

15 See the significant discussion of Erben in these terms in the article by the music critic (and Dvořák partisan) Boleslav Kalenský, in his 'Karel Jaromír Erben', *Dalibor*, vol. 34, no. 3 (1911), pp. 22–4. Kalenský criticizes *Kytice* for its 'erroneous' adherence to *časomíra*.

borrowed from the medieval and modern Latin 'anthologia' or 'florilegium' and before that from the Greek Anthology of the 1st century BC, was common in the Renaissance, and was used in 19th-century Bohemia for collections of poetry linked with music, intended for female readership, the words used being 'věnec', 'kytka', or 'kytice'. The *Věnec ze zpěvů vlastenských* [*A Garland of Patriotic Songs*] of J. K. Chmelenský is a prominent example, a collection of light Czech poetry, 'collected for, and dedicated to, patriotic maidens' [*'uvitý a obětovaný dívkám vlastenským'*], and set to simple music. It was published serially in five volumes between 1835 and 1839, and his *Kytka* also offered poetry suitable for setting to music.[16] Erben's collection of Czech folk-songs from the 1840s is also obviously directed mainly at a female readership; its motto is 'My little daughter! / Just pray / and work and sing!'[17]

In a short introductory poem, Chmelenský apostrophizes his 'patriotic maidens' as the flowers of the nation, who bloom profusely beside the rivers of Bohemia, Moravia and Slovakia, and charmingly match the spring flowers in the garland of songs

---

16 Josef Krasoslav Chmelenský and others, ed., *Wěnec ze zpěwů wlastenských, uwitý a obětowaný djwkám wlastenským s průvodem fortepiana* [*A Garland of Patriotic Songs, Collected for and Dedicated to Patriotic Maidens, with Pianoforte Accompaniment*] (5 vols., Prague: Knjžecj arcibiskupská knihtiskárna, u Josefy Fetterlowé, 1835–9), and idem, ed., *Kytka: dar uměny zpěwu na rok 1837* [*A Bouquet: Gift of the Muses of Song for 1837*] (Prague: W. Špinka, 1836 and subsequent years). Modern edition of the former, with a title underplaying the gendering: Josef Plavec, ed., *Věnec ze zpěvů vlasteneckých: sborník obrozeneckých písní* [*A Garland of Patriotic Songs: A Volume of Songs of the Revival*] (Prague: Státní nakladatelství krásné literatury, hudby a umění, 1960). The composers represented include František Škroup, composer of the music for the Czech national anthem; Chmelenský was also a significant translator of opera libretti.

17 Erben, *Písně národní v Čechách* (see n. 3 above), title page: 'Má dceruško! / - - / Genom se modljwey / A pracug a zpjwey. / Pjseň nár.' The collection of Lusatian folk-songs published by Haupt and Smoleŕ (see n. 13 above) has an equivalent motto.

he is offering them.[18] The same theme, echoed in texts by other poets in Chmelenský's collection, is taken up by Erben in his own short introductory poem, 'The Posy' ['*Kytice*']. Though Erben's garland is presented as modest [*skrovná*], plucked from wilder flowers – the folk poetry, and indeed the 'maternal soul' – of the nation, with Erben there is much greater depth. It is the poems that are apostrophized, not the readers. Even though the mother is long dead, she is the agent, and not her daughters; the motif of loss is paramount; and the gendering is complicated. The first three stanzas present a folk-style legend explaining the origin of the word *mateřidouška* (thyme): the orphaned children of Bohemia, who have been searching daily for their mother, have found wild thyme growing on her grave, and its name recalls the words *matka* (mother) and *duše* (soul). But the legend refers to times long ago and far away: the fourth stanza introduces a fictional author, who has collected these wild flowers 'on an ancient grave-mound' [*na dávné mohyle*], and, uncertain where they should be sent, consigns them as emissaries 'to far-off lands' [*do širých zemí*], where they may be welcomed, perhaps, by some Czech mother's daughter. The implied readers on whom the obligation is laid are again female, young, perhaps orphaned, in

---

18 Chmelenský, *Wěnec ze zpěwů wlastenských* (n. 16 above; here quoted from Plavec, ed., p. 24): 'Vy, jenž vábně břehy obýváte / Labe proudného a Vltavy, / břehy Váhu, Hronu, Moravy, / děvy krásné, vy zpěv z vlasti znáte. / Zazněl' duší Vaší tisíckráte, / jest on medem Vaší zábavy, / i část velké Vaší oslavy, / kterou nejradší se vychloubáte. / Nuže, zde Vám věnec se podává, / uvit z květin písní májových, / tak jak přízeň času je shledává. / Jako ony, Vy jste chlouba naše, / obě dcery krajin rájových; / pějte – pak je každé srdce Vaše.' ['You who charmingly dwell on the banks of the rushing Labe and the Vltava, the banks of the Váh, the Hron, the Morava, fair maidens, you know the song of the motherland. It has resounded a thousandfold in your soul; it is the honey of your diversion, and the part of your great celebration in which you most gladly boast. Here a garland is presented to you, collected from the flowers of the songs of May: it brings them together as a favour of the season. Like [the flowers], you are our boast; you are both daughters of paradisal regions; sing – then [the garland] is each heart of yours.']

exile, and in danger of losing the soul of the nation; the implied author is male, older, and learned. The 'far-off lands' might be the distant regions of Czech- and Slovak-speaking Central Europe, as in Chmelenský – or perhaps Erben has in mind places where the motherland and language might genuinely be forgotten, after the large-scale migration of Czechs to Vienna, and to the USA, that occurred after 1848.[19]

The rest of the collection, too, deals with themes of correct motherhood and correct daughterhood, with punishment inflicted on women who breach the moral code, and authorial warnings issued to those who might be tempted to do so. In 'The Wedding Shirts', the blasphemy in Bürger's 'Lenore' is eliminated, allowing the heroine – again an orphan, and a good Catholic – to 'think on God in time of need' and avoid damnation, though not to avoid the authorial finger-wagging of the last stanza. More unexpected is 'The Daughter's Curse', a dialogue between mother and daughter: the daughter has murdered her infant, but it is the mother who is punished, for having failed to bring her daughter up properly. (This moral links this poem, curiously, with 'Záhoř's Bed', where the action is also the consequence of a parent's error.) The poem is a close parallel to the Scottish ballad 'Edward', one of those in Thomas Percy's collection, from which Erben may have

---

[19] Emigration of Czechs from Bohemia and Moravia is a constant theme from the 18th century onwards, at first usually of servants at aristocratic courts, but the railways and industries such as the Viennese brickworks increasingly attracted Czech migrant labour in the 19th century, and the USA was a destination for both Czechs and Germans, especially after 1848. Estimates of the period suggest that there were around 83,000 Czechs living in Vienna in 1851: see Michael John, ed., *Schmelztiegel Wien – einst und jetzt: Zur Geschichte und Gegenwart von Zuwanderung und Minderheiten, Aufsätze, Quellen, Kommentare* (Vienna and Cologne: Böhlau Verlag, 1990), p. 18, quoted in Monika Glettler, 'Das tschechische Wien historisch', in Christa Rothmeier, ed., *Die entzauberte Idylle: 160 Jahre Wien in der tschechischen Literatur* (Vienna: Verlag der Österreichischen Akademie der Wissenschaften, 2004), pp. 77–108, here quoted from p. 82.

borrowed it, either directly (perhaps in Herder's German translation) or via its reworking in the final act of the play *Maria Stuart* (1832) by the Polish author Juliusz Słowacki.[20] If so, however, the re-gendering of the poem is striking: Percy's and Słowacki's versions are dialogues between mother and son, where the son has murdered his father, and it is the son who must be punished.

It might seem that this implied readership is underplayed or ignored in the groundbreaking essays on Erben published in 1935 and 1936 by Roman Jakobson and Jan Mukařovský, members of the Prague Linguistic Circle [*Pražský lingvistický kroužek*]. These interpret Erben and his contemporary K. H. Mácha, no doubt correctly, as strongly contrasted currents in Czech Romanticism.[21] Mukařovský, in particular, sees one aspect of this opposition in terms of differing masculinities: a maturely 'masculine character' [*mužný ráz*] governs Erben's poetry, whereas Mácha's more nihilistic poetry has the character of adolescent male youth [*jinošství*].[22] But this interpretation of Erben does indeed take

---

20 Juliusz Słowacki, *Maria Stuart: drama historyczne w pięciu aktach* [*Mary Stuart: A Historical Drama in Five Acts*] (Paris: A. Pinard, 1830). In Act V, scene 1, a page recites the ballad 'Edward' 'in a childish voice', with ironic effect. In his biography of Erben (*Karel Jaromír Erben*, n. 5 above), Julius Dolanský argues that Erben's *Kytice* is directly dependent on this and other sources in the poetry of Słowacki; further on this subject, see idem, 'Erben a Słowacki', *Česká literatura*, vol. 19, no. 3–4 (1971), pp. 233–47.

21 Roman Jakobson, 'Poznámky k dílu Erbenovu: I. O mythu' ['Notes on Erben's Work, i: Myth'], *Slovo a slovesnost*, vol. 1, no. 3 (1935), pp. 152–64 (Eng. trans. as 'Notes on myth in Erben's work', in Roman Jakobson, *Language in literature*, ed. Krystyna Pomorska and Stephen Rudy (Cambridge, MA, and London: Belknap Press of Harvard University Press, 1987), pp. 379–96); Jakobson, 'Poznámky k dílu Erbenovu: II. O verši' ['Notes on Erben's Work, ii: Versification'], *Slovo a slovesnost*, vol. 1, no. 4 (1935), pp. 218–29; Jan Mukařovský, 'Protichůdci: Několik poznámek o vztahu Erbenova básnického díla k Máchovu' ['Opposites: Notes on the Relationship of Erben's Poetry to Mácha's'], *Slovo a slovesnost*, vol. 2, no. 1 (1936), pp. 33–43.

22 Mukařovský, 'Protichůdci' (n. 21), at p. 35: 'Mužný ráz *vší* poesie Erbenovy je třeba chápat jako přijatý typ i jako charakteristický ráz básnické struktury Erbenových děl, zcela podobně jako Máchovo jinošství.' (The emphasis is Mukařovský's.)

into account the fictional narrator who comes into focus at the ends of a few of the poems in *Kytice*: the first-person collector of tales in 'The Posy', the religious moralizer in 'The Wedding Shirts', and, especially, the grandpa [*stařeček*] in 'The Treasure', whose voice echoes throughout the collection.

For composers who needed to achieve success by making their voice heard outside the Czech lands, the gendering may well have become problematic later in the century. Antonín Dvořák, for example, composed four symphonic poems in the 1890s, based on four of the *Kytice* poems (mentioned further below). These met with a lukewarm reception with Viennese critics, by contrast with his next symphonic poem, the *Píseň bohatýrská* [*Heroic Song*], op. 111, of 1897, which is far less obviously programmatic or based on literature, though equally patriotic in intention. In part, their critical verdict reflects an assumption that Dvořák, as a protégé of Johannes Brahms, must be an opponent of Franz Liszt (composer of symphonic poems) and Richard Wagner, in the polemical debates current in Vienna at the time. But the assumed gendering of the four earlier compositions may also have influenced the response of Dvořák's Viennese critics. Christopher Campo-Bowen argues that the *Píseň bohatýrská* has an 'obviously masculinized artist-hero program' making it 'more palatable for non-Czech audiences' than the works based on Erben, with their 'easily feminized and othered programs based on supernatural Czech folk tales and revolving around conflicts involving female characters'.[23]

---

23 Christopher Campo-Bowen, 'Bohemian Rhapsodist: Antonín Dvořák's *Píseň bohatýrská* and the Historiography of Czech Music', *19th-Century Music*, vol. 40, no. 2 (2016), pp. 159–81 (this quotation from p. 161).

Cantata, Symphonic Poem, Melodrama

Possibly owing to the difficulty of excerpting lyric texts from the poems of the collection, musical settings of the *Kytice* poems in the Czech lands have favoured dramatic genres – and, astonishingly, there have been very large numbers of such compositions from Erben's own time virtually up to the present day. One of V. J. Tomášek's pupils, Leopold Měchura (1804–70), a prominent composer in the mid-19th century, set 'Christmas Eve' as a cantata in 1866. Further dramatic cantatas from the 1870s and 1880s include works by Alois Hnilička ('The Lily', 1883), Zdeněk Fibich ('Christmas Eve', 1885), and Eugen Miroslav Rutte ('Christmas Eve', 1885), and notably include Dvořák's 'The Wedding Shirts' (1884). The latter marks a newly-kindled interest in Slavonic folklore on the part of the composer, and, written for the Birmingham Festival, also illustrates the favourable reception he received in England. With the English title 'The Spectre's Bride', it is a large-scale work in 18 sections, for soloists, chorus and orchestra; the composer conducted its British premiere in Birmingham in 1885, although it had already been performed in Plzeň [Pilsen].

To the same tradition, though as an innovation that was not imitated by others, belong the four symphonic poems that Dvořák composed in 1896: 'The Water-goblin' op. 107, 'The Noonday Witch' op. 108, 'The Golden Spinning-wheel' op. 109, and 'The Wild Dove' op. 110. (Earlier projects of the composer in the 1890s, to set 'The Golden Spinning-wheel' as a cantata, and to set 'Záhoř's Bed' in some way, were never completed.) The symphonic poems of 1896 are effectively 'songs without words': no text is sung in them, but Dvořák laid out Erben's words under his music while composing the works, and expanded on his intentions in correspondence with the Viennese critic Robert

Hirschfeld.[24] Detailed analyses of all four were published in the journal *Hlídka* in 1896 and 1897 by the composer Leoš Janáček, who conducted the premiere of 'The Wild Dove' in Brno in March 1898.[25]

However, numerous cantatas based on *Kytice* have continued to be produced, including Bohuslav Martinů's 'The Wedding Shirts' H214 I (3/2) (1931–2), Jaroslav Křička's 'The Golden Spinning-wheel' (1943), and four by Pavel Blatný ('The Willow', 1980; 'The Noonday Witch', 1982; 'Christmas Eve', 1983; 'The Water-goblin', 1988). There is also a four-act opera based on 'The Water-goblin', by Boleslav Vomáčka, with a libretto by Adolf Wenig (1934–7).

---

24 Much of the correspondence is translated from Dvořák's 'imperfect' German, and further details are given, in John Clapham, 'Dvořák's Unknown Letters on his Symphonic Poems', *Music & Letters*, vol. 56, no. 3/4 (1975), pp. 277–87. For more recent literature on Dvořák's *Kytice* symphonic poems, see in particular Wolfgang Dömling, 'Mit und ohne Programm: Dvořák und die Idee der Symphonischen Dichtung', in *The Work of Antonín Dvořák (1841–1904): Aspects of Composition – Problems of Editing – Reception*, ed. Jarmila Gabrielová and Jan Kachlík (Prague: Etnologický ústav Akademie věd České republiky, 2007), pp. 78–81; and Clare A. Thornley, '"Dramas without a Stage, Acts without Singers": Rethinking the Symphonic Poems of Antonín Dvořák', PhD dissertation, New York University, 2011).

25 Leoš Janáček, 'České proudy hudební [I]: […] Dr Antonína Dvořáka "Vodník"' ['Czech Musical Currents I: Dr Antonín Dvořák's "The Water-goblin"'], *Hlídka*, vol. 14 (1897), pp. 285–92; 'České proudy hudební II: [...] Dr Antonína Dvořáka "Polednice"', ['Czech Musical Currents II: Dr Antonín Dvořák's "The Noonday Witch "'], *Hlídka*, vol. 14 (1897), pp. 454–9; 'České proudy hudební III: […] Dr Antonína Dvořáka "Zlatý kolovrat"' [...] ['Czech Musical Currents III: Dr Antonín Dvořák's "The Golden Spinning-wheel" [...]'], *Hlídka*, vol. 14 (1897), pp. 594–604; 'České proudy hudební [IV]: […] Holoubek, symfonická báseň pro velký orchestr, složil Antonín Dvořák' ['Czech Musical Currents IV: The Wild Dove, Symphonic Poem for Large Orchestra, composed by Antonín Dvořák'], *Hlídka*, vol. 15 (1898), pp. 277–82. English translations of the articles on 'The Golden Spinning-Wheel' and 'The Wild Dove': Leoš Janáček, 'A Discussion of Two Tone Poems Based on Texts by Karel Jaromír Erben: "The Wood Dove" and "The Golden Spinning Wheel"', in Michael Beckerman, ed., *Dvořák and His World* (Princeton, NJ: Princeton University Press, 1993), pp. 262–76

A more distinctive legacy of *Kytice* and its dramatic style, however, developed in the 'melodrama' (spoken recitation, not sung, accompanied by music, for performance either in the salon or on stage). This marked a conscious revival, and conversion into a distinctive genre, of an 18th-century dramatic device perhaps invented by Jean-Jacques Rousseau (*Pygmalion, c.* 1762). Melodrama was famously employed by the Czech composer Jiří Antonín [Georg Anton] Benda (1722–95), who was still well-known in the 19th century for his melodramas *Ariadne auf Naxos* and *Medea*, both composed for public declamation at the court of Gotha in 1775. The technique was also used by W. A. Mozart, in passages in his *Zaide* (1779–80), and later by Beethoven, Schubert, and numerous others, especially in Vienna, usually for dramatic effect in passages within longer compositions.

The composer Zdeněk Fibich (1850–1900) was especially influential in establishing melodrama as a distinct genre in the Czech sphere, and in popularizing *Kytice* as a source for melodrama texts.[26] He had conducted Jiří Benda's *Ariadne* to mark its centenary in 1875, and he set Erben's 'Christmas Eve' as a concert melodrama for reciter and piano that same year. Among melodramas with texts by other poets, 'The Water-goblin' followed in 1883 for reciter and orchestra, and the two Erben melodramas

---

26 For newer literature on Fibich and his melodramas, see Jaroslav Jiránek, 'Die Semantik des Melodrams: ein Sonderfall der musiko-literarischen Gattungen, demonstriert am Werk Zdeněk Fibichs', in *Die Semantik der musiko-literarischen Gattungen, Methodik und Analyse: eine Festgabe für Ulrich Weisstein zum 65. Geburtstag*, ed. Walter Bernhart (Tübingen: Narr, 1994), pp. 153–73; Judith Ann Mabary, 'Redefining Melodrama: The Czech Response to Music and Word' (PhD dissertation, Washington University, St. Louis, 1999); Jan Smaczny, 'The Operas and Melodramas of Zdeněk Fibich (1850–1900)', *Proceedings of the Royal Musical Association*, vol. 109 (1982–3), pp. 119–33; Patrick F. Devine and others, eds., *Zdeněk Fibich as a Central European Composer at the End of the Nineteenth Century*, Musicologica Olomucensia, vol. 12 (Olomouc: Palacký University, 2010); Věra Šustíková, *Zdeněk Fibich a český koncertní melodram* (Olomouc: Palacký University, 2014).

were deservedly popular. 'The Water-goblin', in particular, a work of Fibich's maturity, has continuous music, divided into four movements following the divisions of the text; the music is developed symphonically, but includes occasional pictorialisms, such as those where the girl sings a lullaby to her infant and the goblin knocks at the door. It deserves to be far better known; Fibich's relative obscurity at the present day may in part be the result of a reaction against the efforts once made to promote him by Zdeněk Nejedlý, ideologue of Stalinism.[27]

Fibich's example was followed by many others in the decades before the First World War: these include *Kytice* melodramas by E. M. Rutte ('The Lily', 1879; 'Christmas Eve', 1907), Karel Kovařovic ('The Golden Spinning-wheel', 1887), Otakar Ostrčil ('The Lily', 1895), Ladislav Basler ('The Lily', 1898), and Alfred Jelínek ('Záhoř's Bed', 1906), besides isolated examples later in the 20th century.

Geoffrey Chew
Egham, November 2019

---

[27] Zdeněk Nejedlý, *Zdenko Fibich, zakladatel scénického melodramatu* (Prague: Hejda & Tuček, 1901).

ORIGINAL EDITIONS OF *KYTICE*
AND PREVIOUS COMPLETE TRANSLATIONS

Karel Jaromír Erben, *Kytice z pověstí národních* (Prague: Jaroslav Pospíšil, 1853; 2nd ed., Prague: Jaroslav Pospíšil, 1861)

Karel Jaromír Erben, 'Баллады : Букет из народных преданий', trans. Nikolai Nikolaevich Aseyev, in Mikhail Zenkevich and Mikhail Golodniy [Czech: Michajl Zenkevič a Michajl Golodnij], eds., *Баллады, стихи, сказки: авторский сборник* (Moscow: Goslitizdat, 1948), pp. 17–125 [includes commentary, pp. 291–301]

Karel Jaromír Erben, *Kytice, un bouquet de légendes tchèques: édition bilingue*, trans. Daniel Larangé, Xavier Galmiche, and others, Cahiers slaves – bohemica, Classiques Tchèques, vol. 4 (Paris: Editions Persée, 2001) [includes a 'Postface: *Un bouquet de Karel Jaromír Erben, l'originalité difficile*' by Xavier Galmiche, pp. 202–15]

Karel Jaromír Erben, *Ein Blumenstrauss mit tschechischer Poesie in deutschen Versen*, trans. Georg Ehrfried Chalupa (Oberursel (Taunus): Grippo, 2011)

Karel Jaromír Erben, *Der Blumenstrauß / Kytice*, trans. Eduard Albert and Marie Kwaysser (Passau: Stutz, 2011)

Karel Jaromír Erben, *A Bouquet of Czech Folktales*, trans. Marcela Malek Sulak (Prague: Twisted Spoon Press, 2012)

Karel Jaromír
Erben
Kytice

The Posy

A mother died, and in the grave they laid her;
    Her orphaned children, left behind,
Came every morning and a visit paid her,
    Seeking their mother dear to find.

For her dear children so the mother grieved
    Her long lost soul once more was found
Embodied in a flower with tiny leaves
    Spreading across her burial-mound.

They knew their mother by its exhalation –
    They knew, and joyful they became;
The simple flower that brought them consolation
    'Mother's dear soul' they chose to name.

Soul of our mother, dear to our own nation,
    You simple narratives of ours,
On that far mound I plucked your inspiration –
    Whom shall I give of these flowers?

Into a modest posy I will bind you,
    With ornamental ribbon wound;
To far-flung lands a pathway I will find you
    Where people of your kin abound.

And there, perhaps, the daughter of some mother
    Will draw the sweet breath of your scent;
Perhaps the son of someone or another
    You'll meet, his heart on you intent.

The Treasure

I

 Amongst the beech-trees, on a mound,
A little church, low-towered, stood;
And from the tower was heard a sound
In hamlet close at hand, and wood.
The church bell's sound is nothing choice,
Lost on nearby hillsides falling:
Dark is the clapper's wooden voice,
Folk to God's own temple calling.

 From the hamlet, God revering,
Crowds of people make their way;
These are village folk, God-fearing,
And Good Friday falls today

 In church it's gloomy: walls stripped bare,
The altar with a black veil hung;
A cross stands firm upon it there;
In the choir the Passion's sung.

 But see – what is that flash of white
In the black woods beyond the spring?
Some woman from the hamlet, she –
Who in her arms holds something tight.

With rapid steps she's hastening,
Dressed in her Sunday finery,
There on the slope beyond the spring –
A little boy she's holding tight.
The woman's running; down she flies,
To God's own temple hurrying by:
There on the wooded slope nearby
The church upon its hillock lies.
And in the dale towards the spring,
Sharply her steps she's quickening;
For the freely-blowing breezes
Sounds of song from church are bringing:
Of the Passion of Lord Jesus
In the choir just now they're singing.
She runs – beside the rock she flies:
'Can I believe my eyes? Strange thing…
What, are my senses telling lies?'
She stops, and all around her stares –
Rapidly her steps retraces,
Stops again; about she faces –
'The forest's there, the brushwood's here,
And through the fields the path leads there –
I can't have lost my way, that's clear!
What's happening to me, Lord – what's wrong?
Why is that stone not here by me?
Whatever is this change I see?'
Again she stops, again walks on,
She goes, all incredulity,
Her eyes she's rubbing with her hand;
She moves, and one step nearer stands:
'Dear God, what change is this I see?'

Where, from wild brushwood overgrown,
From the church three hundred paces,
In the path jutted one great stone,
What's the sight her eye now faces?
There before her, plain as plain –
The hill gapes wide, an entrance clear –
Something that she can't explain –
The stone stands in the pathway here,
The whole rock planted firm, four-square,
As if it always had been there.
To the woman's eyes is shown
A way beneath the earth, a room
Vaulted in the flinty stone;
Where the vaulted hall's concealed
In the hillock's sombre womb,
Something like a flame's revealed.
And it burns with shining whiteness
Like the moon's clear glow at night;
And it flames with crimson brightness,
Like the sunset's western light.

The woman, seeing this, amazed,
A step towards the entrance tries;
Using her palm to shade her eyes,
She looks around this radiant place.
'Lord, how it shines in here – how bright!'
Her eyes she's rubbing with her hand;
She moves, and one step nearer stands:
'How it shines here – how strangely bright!
Whatever can it be, that light?'
But she's afraid to venture more,
And stands outside; looks through the door.

    She lingers, standing by the door –
No longer in the vault she stays;
As fear within her gaze is quelled,
By curiosity impelled,
Onward the woman makes her way.
Step after step – and all the way,
Stronger is every one she takes;
Step after step – through rock of grey
Where only a sleeping echo wakes.
As further on the woman goes,
The curious radiance grows apace.
The vault comes to an end just there,
But such astonishment she shows
That with her hand she hides her face,
She cannot risk a direct stare.
She sees – what is she seeing, then?
Whoever saw the like, and when?
Such beauty and such brilliancy
In heaven alone she thought to see!

    Open wide, the door's revealing
Such a hall, resplendent, grand;
Bright with gold the walls are gleaming,
Set with rubies is the ceiling;
Below it, crystal pillars stand.
Then, on both sides of the door –
None would believe, had they not seen –
Upon a polished marble floor
Two fires are burning, bright and keen;
Yes, two bright fires are burning there,
Nothing can quench their brilliant flare:

Above the silver, from the heights,
On the left the moon's fire shimmers;
Above the gold, upon the right,
Ceaselessly the sun's fire glimmers.
The fires blaze bright, the room's ablaze,
Veiled in a radiance pure and clear;
And all the time the treasure stays,
The flames are not extinguished here,
Nothing can quench their brilliant flare.

   The woman on the threshold stays,
She stands quite blind, deprived of sight;
She's too afraid her eyes to raise,
She cannot watch the blazing light.
With her left hand she holds the child,
And with the right rubs her left eye;
When she has looked around a while,
Remembers, and fresh courage takes,
And then she heaves a deep, deep sigh,
And inwardly deliberates:
'Dear God, what hunger and what need
As trials in this world I must bear!
A wretched life I have to lead –
And so much treasure over there!
Gold and silver, such a lot,
Lie here hidden underground!
Just a pinch from all that's piled –
I'd be rich with what I'd got;
I'd be the happiest one around,
And, along with me, my child!'

Reflecting, standing at a loss,
Her sense of danger grows and grows;
Protected by the holy cross
She moves to where the white flame glows.
She goes a silver piece to take,
But there she lays it down again;
Picks it up to contemplate
Its glitter, and to test its weight –
And does she lay it down again?
No, in her lap a flash it makes.
Bolder with this success she grows:
'Here in this God's finger's plain –
The treasure's hiding-place he showed,
He wants to shower me with bliss:
I should sin, his grace abusing,
If his gift I were refusing!'

   As to herself she's saying this,
She puts her small boy down again;
She kneels, and spreads her lap out – see,
From the heaps scoops eagerly,
In her lap the silver piling:
'Here in this God's finger's plain,
he wills it – on us fortune's smiling!'
And from the heaps takes more and more –
Scarce can stand, lap overflowing,
Yet more in her skirts she's stowing,
Deceived by silver's false allure!
But when she has a mind to leave –
Ah, there is still her little son!
How can she, with such weight to heave?

He's only two, the little one;
Her fortune back again to shake
Is not a good plan, she believes,
But both of them she cannot take.

    See, the silver mother's taking!
After her he trots, legs shaking:
"Mama!" calling, "Mama! mama!"
Small hands clutch with tearful clamour.
'Hush, there, sonny, hush, hush, child, now!
Wait there just a little while now,
She'll be back at once, will mama!'

    From the hall she's running, flying,
Now the hall's behind her lying;
Over the stream, to the wood, uphill,
The woman hastens, joyful still.
And when a little while has passed,
Empty-handed, back she hurries,
Scarcely breathing, sweating, flurried,
To reach her goal again at last.

    As they softly blow, the breezes
From the church a song are bringing:
Of the Passion of Lord Jesus
In the choir just now they're singing.

    As she enters from the hall:
"Ha, ha, mama! Ha, ha, mama!"
with happy smiles her child does call,
clapping hands with joyful clamour.

But not at all does mother care –
To the far side she goes dashing,
She prefers the metal's flashing;
Gold, dearest of all metals there.
She kneels and spreads her lap out – see,
From the heaps scoops eagerly;
In her lap the gold she's piling;
Scarce can stand, lap overflowing –
Yet more in her skirts she's stowing!
How her heart with joy is leaping,
At her fortune how she's smiling!

As the gold his mother's taking,
After her the child, legs shaking,
Toddles, piteously weeping:
"Mama, mama! Oh, oh, mama!" –
Small hands clutch with tearful clamour.
'Hush, my sonny, hush, hush, child, now,
wait for just a little while now.'
To the baby stooping down,
In her lap her hand she's dipping;
Out of it two coins she's slipping,
Coin from coin strikes ringing sounds:
'Look what mama's got, my impling!
Chink, chink! Can you hear it tinkling?'
Though the child still goes on weeping,
Her own heart with joy is leaping.

In her lap again she's dipping;
Out a heap of gold comes slipping –
In his lap the gold she's sprinkling –
'Look what mama's got, my impling!

Hush, my sonny, hush, hush, child, now:
Chink, chink! Listen to it tinkling!
Wait here just a little while now,
Mama's coming in a twinkling.
Come, play nicely, lad, with it –
Wait for just a little bit.'

    From the hall she's running, flying,
Not a backward glance she's sparing;
Now the hall's behind her lying,
Now towards the brook she's tearing;
Across the brook, uphill, with pleasure,
To the wood, her precious treasure
To the cottage now she's bearing.

    'Hey there, cottage, mean and poor,
Soon to you I'll say goodbye!
Do I need you any more?
You've no charm to catch my eye!
I'll quit these forests dark and bleak,
Father's poor roof left behind me,
Somewhere else my fortune seek,
Somewhere else to live I'll find me!
From this countryside I'm going –
I'll be glad to get away –
Where my fortune ripe is growing,
To the city make my way.
Castles and estates I'll buy,
A lady's rank to me they'll give:
Cottage, time to say goodbye –
In you I'll no longer live!

I'm not that poor widow now,
Night and day weighed down with care;
Look here, in my lap,' – see how
She looks down with rapture there.
Oh, if only she'd refrained!
She's pale with terror, colour drained;
Pure terror makes her shake and sway –
It's strange she doesn't faint away.
She sees – she sees – what does she see?
Her own eyes she's scarcely trusting!
To the cracked old door she's thrusting,
To the place where stood the chest
In which the silver's laid to rest.
Lifts the lid – what does she see?
By all good folks' piety!
What can this be – ah, what new blow?
Instead of silver, stones lie stored;
In skirts and lap all stowed away –
Oh, terrible, uncanny fraud!
Instead of gold there's only clay!
All her hopes are trampled low.

    Undeserved good luck possessing,
She did not enjoy its blessing.

II

And as this crushing fact appears,
She registers her loss, appalled,
Sharp pain the woman's heart does pierce;
She screams aloud in terror fierce,
She screams to shake the cottage walls:
'Oh, my child! My child, my darling!'
"Child, my darling – darling – darling!"
the forest thick in echo calls.

By terrible foreboding gnawed,
The woman runs – ah, no, she's flying,
Flying like a bird in flight,
Through woods and hills she comes in sight,
To where she found the treacherous hoard,
The hillock where the church is lying.

Why no song now are they bringing,
Blowing from the church, those breezes?
Of the Passion of Lord Jesus
In the choir no more they're singing.

When to the vault she's drawing nigh,
Ha! – what a sight there meets her eye!
Ha! – from wild brushwood overgrown,
From the church three hundred paces,
There in the path juts one great stone!

And where's the hall? Clean gone – no traces!
Gone – and the rock stands in the way,
As if it never was away.

    Ha – what fear the woman's feeling,
How in alarm she calls and seeks!
Round the hillock roaming, reeling
Through brushwood, pale as death her cheeks.
With despairing eyes she rushes,
With corpse-like pallor, livid lips!
See her run through those wild bushes,
Running – to the ground she slips.
'It's not here – oh, woe, oh, pain!'
Body by rough brushwood torn,
Feet pierced through and through by thorns –
But all her knocking is in vain,
The entrance can't be found again!

    The woman's seized by fresh despair
Gripped by dreadful agony:
'Who'll give back my child to me?
Oh, my child, where are you, where?'

    "Deep beneath the ground – I'm here!"
a soft voice murmurs on the breeze,
"No one understands – no ear,
there's no watchful eye that sees."

    "What fun underground, what fun,
With no drink and with no pap,
On the floor – a marble one! –
Pure gold in my little lap!"

"There's no change from night to day,
Not an eye in sleep is winking:
I'm playing nicely here, I play –
Chink, chink! Can you hear it chinking?"

But she searches on – no good!
Yet again she's racked with fear,
On the ground she writhes, despairing,
From her head the hair she's tearing,
Deathly pale and stained with blood:
'Woe, ah, woe! Oh, if I could –
Child, where are you, where, my dear,
can I find my child, my darling?'
"Child, my darling – darling – darling!"
echoes from the forests near.

III

One day goes by; another's past,
Days into a week are turning,
A month from weeks unfolds at last,
And summer's heat begins its burning.

Among the beech-trees, on a mound,
The little church, low-towered, stood,
And every day its bell did sound
In hamlet close at hand, and wood.
There, when the bell is summoning
Early when mass is being said,
Before the temple of Heaven's King
The pious peasant bows his head.

Who knows her – face bowed to the ground,
That person bending low in prayer?
The altar candles have burned down,
But still she goes on kneeling there.
She's not breathing, it appears –
Cheeks and lips are colourless –
She prays so quietly no-one hears!
Who? I don't know; I can guess…
When, later, after holy mass,
The church's door is locked behind her,
Among the beeches see her pass,
Going down the hill you'll find her.

Slowly, slowly she makes her way,
A track that winds where brushwood's grown,
There, up to that rock of grey,
Where in the path juts one great stone.
Then she heaves a deep, deep sigh,
On her palms her forehead leaning:
'Oh, my child!' – and now her eye
Drowns in tears, in torrents streaming.

   That cottage woman's never glad,
Forever sunk in thought so deep,
 She's always pale, and always sad,
From daybreak to when twilight dies
No brightness ever in her eyes;
At night, her grief gives her no sleep.
And when once more at earliest dawn
She leaves her bed of misery:
'My child, my darling child forlorn!
Oh, woe is me, oh woe!' she weeps.
'Oh, gracious Lord, please pardon me!'

   Autumn's gone, and winter's ceased –
Now a whole year has gone by;
In her heart, grief's unappeased,
And from her eyes tears never die.
And when on high the sun did soar,
New warmth to the earth supplying,
Her mouth to smile was warmed no more –
Still the widow went on crying.

IV

Hark! From up among the beeches,
From that church, its tower not high,
Rattling clangour once more reaches
Villages and woods nearby.
From the hamlet, God revering,
See crowds hurrying up this way;
These are village folk, God-fearing,
And Good Friday falls today.

Gently blow the soft spring breezes,
On the wind a song they're bringing:
In the church once more they're singing
Of the Passion of Lord Jesus.

Out of the woods she makes her way,
Downhill, towards the stream in spate.
What's slowing down her steps today?
Her last year's memories of this day
Her steps with bitter sorrow weight.
Little by little, she draws near,
And now beside the rock appears.

See – what sight her eye now faces?
There, from wild brushwood overgrown,
From the church three hundred paces,
Out in the path juts one great stone:
The hill gapes wide, an entrance clear,

The stone stands in the pathway here,
The stone and that whole rock, four-square,
As if it always had been there.

   At this the woman's so dismayed,
That all her hairs in terror rise;
With all its weight upon her lies
Her sorrow – and her guiltiness.
She does not wait, though she's afraid,
And full of hope and of distress,
Bounding towards that hall she flies,
Well-known, below the rocks at hand.

   See the open door, revealing
Such a hall, resplendent, grand:
With pure gold the walls are gleaming,
Set with rubies is the ceiling;
Beneath it, crystal pillars stand.
Two bright fires are flickering
There on each side of the door,
Upon a polished marble floor:
Above the silver, from the heights,
On the left the moon's fire shimmers;
Above the gold, upon the right,
Ceaselessly the sun's fire glimmers.

   The woman now draws close in fear
And full of hope and of distress,
All round the chamber see her peer.
Might silver charm, or gold allure her? –
Ah, now they've no attraction for her!
'Ha, ha, mama! Ha, ha, mama!'

See – her child, her own, no less,
Lamented for a whole long year,
Claps his hands with joyful clamour.

   But the woman gasps for air,
Head to foot with terror shaking,
And with speed born of sheer despair,
Tight in her arms the child she packs,
And far off from the hall she's taking.

   Crash, crash! A roaring at her back –
On her heels, in the mountain's womb;
A howling gale, a dreadful crack,
The earth is trembling, noise and row –
Back there, the hall's collapsing – boom!
'Mother of God, ah, help me now!'
In agony the woman calls,
As she looks back in fear, appalled.

   See what a change once more befalls!
All's silent; where the brushwood's grown,
There in the path juts one great stone;
All's as before, with nothing wrong,
No signs the way inside record:
That very moment ends the song
That hymns the Passion of Our Lord.

   But the woman gasps for air,
Head to foot with terror shaking;
And with speed born of sheer despair,
Far away her child she's taking;

To her breast the child she's crushing
As if she feared another shock,
With scarcely breath to run, she's rushing
Till far behind her lies the rock.
She runs, and never once looks back,
Close to the woods, there on the hill,
In terror and delight, until
She stops in her poor forest shack.

   What thanks the woman fervently
Offers to her Creator now!
What streams of tears are flowing – see!
Look how her child she's holding tight,
Kissing his little hands, lips, brow;
And once more to her bosom wraps,
How she is floating in delight!

   Look – what's that shining in his lap?
What is that ringing? Why, pure gold!
That gold with which her child had played,
And which, a year ago, she'd tossed,
And in his little lap she'd laid.

   But on the woman, its charm's lost,
For how much sorrow it has cost!
It cost her, ah! so many a tear;
But, thanking God for this, she holds
Her dear child close with longing there.
This she has learnt through grief and fear:
That, though there's little worth in gold,
A child's is high beyond compare!

V

Down, long since, that church did tumble;
Silent now the bell's clear calling;
Where the beeches stood, now falling
Over rotten roots you stumble.

So much the old man can recall,
And much of it ripe for the grave,
Still, folk seem happy, after all,
A place for him, for now, to save.

When the young ones sit together
Of an evening cold and hoary,
Gladly he will tell the story
Of the widow and the treasure.

The Wedding Shirts

The clock had struck eleven at night,
And still the lamp was shining bright;
And still the lamp was burning clear
Over the prie-dieu hanging near.

A picture of God's Mother hung
– God's Mother with her little son –
upon the wall of that low room;
a rosebud with a rose in bloom.

Before the almighty Virgin there
A girl was kneeling, deep in prayer;
Head bowed, in supplication lost;
Upon her breast her hands lay crossed;
The tears were falling from her eyes;
Her bosom heaved with anguished sighs.
Each tear that dropped fell down to rest
And disappeared on that white breast.

'Where is my father now, alas?
Over his body grows the grass!
Alas, where is my mother, where?
She's lying by my father there!
My sister died within the year;
A bullet killed my brother dear.

I had a sweetheart, to my sorrow;
I would have died for him tomorrow!
To foreign lands he went away,
And hasn't come back to this day.

He went away to foreign lands,
And dried my tears with soothing hands:
"Now sow some flax-seed, darling, see,
and every day, remember me.
The first year, set about the spinning;
The second, damp and bleach the linen;
And sew shirts when the third's beginning:
And when those shirts are finished, you
Shall weave yourself a crown of rue."

It's finished; all the shirts I sewed
Are safely in my hope-chest stowed.
My crown's already dry and sere,
And still my sweetheart isn't here.
Out in the wide, wide world is he –
A stone lost deep beneath the sea.
Three years since news of him arrived –
God only knows if he's alive!

O Virgin Mary, rich in power,
Support me – help me in this hour:
Bring back my love from foreign parts,
The one flower to rejoice my heart.
Bring back my sweetheart from abroad,
Or cut my life and sufferings short:
With him, my life's a flower in spring –
Without, the world's a frozen thing.

O Mary, mother of relief,
Bring help and comfort in my grief!'

The picture moved upon the wall –
The girl cried out in fear, appalled;
The lamp, whose flame was burning weakly,
Sputtered, and then went out completely.
A draught of wind that blew it out? –
A sign that evil was about?

Hark! On the porch a footfall came,
And tap! tap! on the window-frame –
'Are you awake or sleeping, dear?
Hey there, my lass – it's me, I'm here!
Hey there, lass – what are you about?
Do you still know me – not a doubt?
Or has another cut me out?'

'My sweetheart! Oh, by heaven above!
I've just been thinking of you, love;
I've thought about you every day;
For you – this moment! – I did pray.'

"Ha, leave your praying – let it be!
Jump to it – come and follow me;
The moon is shining as our guide,
And I have come to fetch my bride."

'What do you mean? For heaven's sake!
Where should we go? It's far too late!
The night is bleak, the wind blows strong –
Wait until day – it isn't long.'

"Ha, night is day, and day is night –
Dreams weigh my eyes down when it's light!
Before the cockerels awake,
You as my own bride I must take.
Jump to it, now, and don't delay,
you'll be my wife this very day!"

It was the deepest hour of night,
The moon was shining from the heights,
The village was all silent, bleak,
But for the stormy wind's wild shriek.

By leaps and bounds he went ahead,
And after him the girl did tread.
The dogs were howling as they went,
As they picked up the travellers' scent;
They howled and howled – a curious cry,
To say a dead man was nearby!

"A fine, clear night – about this time,
out of their graves the dead do climb,
before you know it, they are near –
my darling, do you feel no fear?"

'What should I fear? You're by my side,
and God's eye watches far and wide.
But come along, my darling, tell –
Your father, is he alive and well?
Your father and your mother sweet –
Will she be happy when we meet?'

"You want to know a lot, my dear!
Come quickly – all will soon be clear.
Come quickly, now – time will not stay,
Before us lies a long, long way.
Love, what's that in your right hand there?"

'I've brought some little books of prayers.'

"Throw them away! Those prayers and moans
are heavier than so many stones!
Throw them away to travel light
And keep in step with me tonight."

The little books he seized and threw,
And at one bound ten miles they flew.

Through high lands now their journey wound,
With rocks and desolate woods all round;
In gullies and on cliff-tops stark
They heard wild bitches yelp and bark.
The tawny owl with hooting cry
Announced ill-fortune was close by.

By leaps and bounds he went ahead
And after him the girl did tread.
On rocks and briars' thorny stalks
Those feet of hers, so white, now walked.
And on the flints and underwood
They left behind a trail of blood.

"A fine, clear night – just now, they say,
the dead among the living stray;
Before you know it, they are near –
My darling, do you feel no fear?"

'What should I fear? You're by my side,
and God's hand shelters far and wide.
But come along, my darling, tell –
What is your house like? Furnished well?
A nice clean parlour? Bright and gay?
And is the church not far away?'

"You want to know a lot, my dear!
This very day, all will be clear.
Come quickly, now, because time flies –
A long way still before us lies-
Love, what's that round your waist I see?"

'I've brought along my rosary.'

"That rosary of bladder-nuts
Twists round you like a snake, and cuts
Your breath with coils that pinch and bruise.
Throw it away – no time to lose!"

The rosary he snatched and threw:
At one bound twenty miles they flew.

Through lowlands now their journey wound,
Through water, meadows, swampy ground;
And in the swamps and caverns too,

Will-o'-the-wisps played, gleaming blue:
A double file, nine in each row,
As when with a corpse to the grave they go.
And by the stream a noisy throng
Of frogs croaked out a funeral song.

    By leaps and bounds he went ahead,
She followed, now with weaker tread.
The grasses, with their sharp-edged blades,
Slashed at the feet of that poor maid,
The fresh green ferns on either side
With her own blood were stained and dyed.

    "A fine, clear night – just now, you know,
Swift to their graves the living go;
Before you know, the grave is near –
My darling, do you feel no fear?"

    'I'm not afraid – you're by my side,
and God's will governs far and wide.
But halt a while in this fierce pace,
And let me have a breathing-space.
My spirit's weak, my legs are failing,
And pain like knives my heart impaling!'

    "Just come along, my girl – make haste;
We'll soon be there – no time to waste.
The feast is ready, guests await,
And like an arrow, time flies straight –
What are you wearing on that string,
Around your neck, upon that string?"

'A cross my mother left, poor thing.'

"Ha – that damned bit of gold, you mean,
Has cutting edges sharp and keen!
It pricks you – does the same to me,
Drop it, and like a bird you'll be!"

The little cross he grabbed and threw;
At one bound thirty miles they flew.

There, amid broad and barren lands,
A high and lofty building stands;
Narrow its windows – long, as well,
And on its roof a tower and bell.

"Hey there, my girl – at last we're here!
Can you see anything, my dear?"

'That church, perhaps? God save us all!'

"A church? No – that's my castle hall!"

'That graveyard – crosses, row on row?'

"My garden! Those aren't crosses – no!
Hey there, my darling – look at me:
Over this wall leap merrily!"

'Leave me alone! Oh, let me be!
You're wild and terrible to see;
Fetid as poison is your breath,
Your heart as icy hard as death!'

"My darling, there's no need to fear!
My home's all merriment and cheer:
There's meat aplenty – no blood, though,
Tonight's the first time it's been so!
What's in that bundle there, my own?"

'Those are the shirts that I have sewn.'

"Of those you won't need more than two:
that's one for me, and one for you."

Laughing, he tossed the bundle hence
Onto a grave beyond the fence.
"Now look at me, don't fear at all –
jump after it across that wall."

'But all this way you've gone ahead;
I followed on this path of dread;
You've gone before me up till now:
So jump, and once more show me how!'

With one swift bound he leapt the wall –
No thought of treachery at all;
He leapt five fathoms in the air –
And could not see her anywhere:
Except for when her dress of white
Flickered around her in her flight,
And now a shelter was close by
The evil host could not descry!

A little room stood there – a hut:
The low door with a bolt was shut.
Behind the girl the door slammed fast;
The bolt would keep her safe at last.
The shed was plain – no windows, too;
Between the slats the moon gleamed through;
Tight as a cage, this little shed;
There, on a plank, a man lay – dead.

And what a noise! Outside, there raves
A host of monsters from the graves;
They murmur as they clatter about;
This is the song that they whine out:

"The corpse belongs in the grave's dark hole,
woe to him who neglects his soul!"

And then – upon the door: boom, boom!
He's thundering outside, her groom:
"Come on, dead fellow – stand up, hey!
Draw back that bolt for me, I say!"

The dead man's eyes are open wide;
The dead man rubs them, side to side,
His head half-raising from the ground,
He gathers strength, and looks around.

'Lord God, assist me in this hour,
don't give me into Satan's power!-
Dead man, lie down, and do not rise –
God grant you rest in Paradise!'

The dead man lowered his head once more,
And closed his eyes, just as before.

And there it goes again – boom, boom!
Harder than ever knocks her groom:
"Come on, dead fellow – stand up, hey!
Open this room for me, I say!"

And at that voice, and at that row,
Up from the plank the corpse stands now,
And with stiff arm points to the door –
There where the bolt holds it secure.

'Oh, save my soul, Lord Jesus Christ!
Have mercy when my need is highest!
Dead man, lie down, and do not stand;
God hold us both within his hand!'

The dead man settled down once more,
And stretched his limbs, just as before.

Again – boom, boom! outside they hear;
The girl is blind and deaf with fear!
"Come on, dead fellow – stand up, hey!
Give me that living girl, I say!"

Oh, poor, poor girl! For at those words
He rises one more time – the third;
His great dim eyes roll in his head,
Upon the girl, with fright half-dead.

'Stand by me, Virgin Mary – plead
With your dear Son, and intercede!
I prayed a prayer that was not fitting:
Forgive the sin I was committing!
Oh, free me, Mary, Mother of grace
From the evil forces in this place.'

And close by, in the hamlet, hear –
A cock begins to crow, quite near,
And from the village all around
Whole companies of cocks resound.

The corpse, as he had risen before,
Suddenly sprawled upon the floor,
And all was quiet outside the room –
The crowd had fled – and her evil groom.

As folk are going to early mass,
They stand astonished as they pass:
Up there, one grave is gaping wide,
and in the dead-house stands a bride,
and, upon every burial mound,
shreds of new shirts are scattered round.

Maiden, you showed good sense indeed,
To think on God in time of need,
And from your evil groom were freed!
If you'd tried any other means,
Damned evermore you would have been:
Your graceful body, white and pure,
Would have been like those shirts, for sure!

The Noonday Witch

By the bench there stood an infant,
    Screaming, screaming, loud and wild;
'Can't you just be quiet an instant?
    Hush, you nasty gipsy-child!'

'Now it's noon, or just about,
    Daddy's coming home for dinner:
while I cook, the fire's gone out –
    all your fault, you little sinner!'

'Hush! Your cart's here, your hussar –
    look, your cockerel! – Go on, play!'
Crash, bang! Soldier, cock and cart
    To the corner fly away.

Once again that fearful bellow –
    'May a hornet come and sting you!
Hush, you naughty little fellow,
    Or the Noonday Witch I'll bring you!'

'Come for him, you Noonday Witch, then!
    Come and take this pest for me!' –
In the door into the kitchen,
    Someone softly turns the key.

Little, brown-skinned, strange of feature,
    On her head a kerchief pinned;

With a stick – crook-legged creature,
    Voice that whistles like the wind!

"Give that child here!" 'Lord, forgive
    this sinner's sins, my Saviour dear!'
It's a wonder she still lives,
    For see – the Noonday Witch is here!

Silent as a shadow wreathes,
    The witch towards the table's slipping:
Mother, fearful, scarcely breathes,
    In her lap the child she's gripping.

Twisting round, she looks behind her –
    Poor, poor child – ah, what a fate!
Closer creeps the witch to find her,
    Closer – now she's there – too late!

Now for him her hand is grasping –
    Tighter squeeze the mother's arms:
'For Christ's precious torments!' gasping,
    She sinks senseless with alarm.

Listen – one, two, three and more:
    The noonday bell is ringing clear;
The handle clicks, and as the door
    Flies wide open, father's here.

Child clasped to her breast, he found,
    Lying in a faint, the mother;
He could hardly bring her round,
    But the little one was – smothered.

The Golden Spinning-wheel

I

Around the woods, broad acres lie;
  A lord comes riding, riding by.
He rides a fiery jet-black steed,
Whose shoes ring merrily indeed,
  And all alone he rides.

Dismounting at a cottage – hop!
  He knocks upon the door – clop, clop!
'Hello there! Open up, I say!
Out hunting, I have lost my way.
  Give me water, do!'

Out comes a girl, a flower so fair
  She has no equal anywhere.
She fetches water from the spring;
Sits at her distaff, modest thing,
  Spinning, spinning flax.

There stands the lord, thoughts all awry,
  Forgetting that his mouth is dry.
So fine and straight the thread she plies,
He cannot turn away his eyes
  From the fair spinning-maid.

'Now if your heart and hand are free,
my wedded wife you'll surely be!'
He draws the maiden to his side –
"Ah, sir, I really can't decide
without my mother's will."

'Where is your mother, maiden fair?
I cannot see her anywhere.' –
"My stepmother comes home, good sir,
tomorrow, and her girl with her,
for they have gone to town."

II

Around the woods, broad acres lie;
Once more the lord comes riding by;
He rides a fiery jet-black steed,
Whose shoes ring merrily indeed,
Straight to the cottage door.

Dismounting at the cottage – hop!
He knocks upon the door: clop, clop!
'Hey, open up, good folk, for me,
So that my eyes may quickly see
My own heart's delight!'

Out comes a hag, all skin and bone;
"What brings this fine guest?' cries the crone.
'I bring some news to change your life:
I want your daughter for my wife –
    your stepdaughter, I mean, not."

"Aha, my lord! That's very strange!
Who could have thought of such a change?
Welcome, fine guest – we're glad you came;
But sir – we do not know your name.
    How did you reach us here?"

'Your lord and king I am; this way
blind fortune called me yesterday.
I'll give you gold and silver too;
Your daughter's all I ask of you –
    The pretty spinning-maid.'

"That's stranger still, my lord and king!
Who could have dreamed of such a thing?
We're not grand folk, Your Majesty;
I wish that we could worthier be
    Of your exalted grace!"

"And yet – I love my stepchild so –
I'd sooner let my own girl go;
They're so alike, it's rightly said,
As two eyes in a single head;
    And her thread is silk!"

'Old woman, evil things you've planned!
　Now carry out what I command:
Tomorrow, at the break of day,
Bring your stepdaughter all the way
　　To my royal hall.'

III

"Get up, my girl – it's time to go;
　the king is waiting – drink will flow!
I never thought to see this day:
God grant you safety on your way
　　To the royal hall!"

'Get dressed, my sister dear, get dressed!
　The royal castle's full of guests.
You've set your sights so high, you see,
You've left behind poor humble me –
　　But all the same – fare well!'

"Dornička, hurry – come along,
　for fear your lord should take it wrong;
when you arrive beyond the wood,
then you'll forget your home for good –
　　come now, quickly, come!"

'Mother, dear mother, tell me, do –
why have you brought that knife with you?'
"A knife's good: where cold shadow lies,
I'll gouge out evil serpents' eyes –
    Come now, quickly, come!"

'Sister, dear sister, tell me, do –
why have you brought that axe with you?'
"An axe is good: among the whins
I'll hack off some fierce creature's shins –
    Come now, quickly, come!"

Close to the thickets cold they drew:
    "'Ha, you're the snake – the beast is you!'"
The hills and valleys wept to see
Two women act so cruelly
    To one wretched girl.

"And now, enjoy your lord the king –
    delight in him like anything!
Embrace his lusty body now,
And gaze upon his clear, smooth brow –
    Pretty spinning-maid!"

'Oh, mother, what am I to do?
    What of these eyes – and these legs, too?'
"Don't leave them by the body; then
someone might put them back again –
    better bring them along."

When to the forest's edge they came:
"Nothing to fear, my girl – no shame!
You're as alike, it's rightly said,
As two eyes in a single head –
    No, don't be afraid!"

And as they reached the royal town,
    From the window the king was looking down;
He met them there, walked at their side,
Welcomed the mother and the bride,
    No thought of treachery.

The wedding came – ripe fruit of crime;
    The virgin bride laughed all the time;
And there was merrymaking, feasting
Music and dancing without ceasing,
    All for seven days.

But on the eighth, at break of day,
    The king to war was called away:
'Now fare you well, my own dear bride,
to bitter combat I must ride,
    against our enemies.

'But when I'm back again from war,
    our love's sweet flower will bloom once more;
and, faithful to my memory,
take up your spinning-wheel for me –
    spin busily at home!'

IV

Deep in the forest desolate,
What was that poor young maiden's fate?
Six open springs were flowing fast;
From them her life streamed out at last,
Down on the soft green moss.

Her happiness and strength were fled;
Now death's grim night had come instead;
Her body's cold, blood flows no more –
Ah, pity, pity, sorrow sore –
Oh, if the king had seen!

There in the woods, mid rock and scree,
There lived an old man, strange to see,
Down to his knees a grey beard drifting;
The body on his shoulders lifting,
He bore it to his cave.

'Get up, my lad, take to your heels,
go, fetch the golden spinning-wheel;
and sell it at the royal hall,
but for no other price at all
except a pair of feet.'

Down in the gateway sat the lad;
A golden spinning-wheel he had.
Out of the window the queen did peep:
"Oh, that the wheel were mine to keep,
    all of solid gold!"

"Go down, mother, ask for me
how much that spinning-wheel might be?" –
'It's not dear, my lady – buy!
My father hasn't priced it high:
    It will cost two feet.'

"Feet! A curious price to name!
But I want it, all the same;
Go to my chamber, up the stair;
Dora's feet, mother, you'll find there –
    Give them to the boy."

The youngster took the feet, and then
Back to the woods he ran again.
'Lad, bring the living-water charm
To make this body free from harm,
    Just as it used to be.'

Wound onto wounded limb he drew,
And in each foot life blazed anew;
The body healed, grew into one,
Whole, as if harm was never done,
    All without a flaw.

'Now fetch, my lad – bestir yourself! –
   that golden distaff from the shelf,
and sell it at the royal hall,
but for no other price at all
   except a pair of hands.'

Down in the gateway sat the lad;
   The distaff in his arms he had.
Out of the window the queen did peep:
"Oh, if that distaff were mine to keep,
   to match the spinning-wheel!"

"Stand on the threshold, mother – see
   how much the distaff's price might be?"
'It's not dear, my lady – buy!
My father hasn't priced it high –
   It will cost two hands.'

"Hands! A stranger price to name!
   But I want it, all the same;
Go to my chamber, up the stair –
Dora's hands, mother, you'll find there;
   Bring them here for him."

The youngster took the hands, and then
   Back to the woods he ran again.
'Lad, bring the living-water charm
to make this body free from harm,
   just as it used to be.'

The Golden Spinning-wheel

Wound onto wounded limb he drew,
    And in each hand life blazed anew;
The body healed, grew into one,
Whole, as if harm was never done,
    All without a flaw.

'Jump to it, boy, get on your way!
    A golden cone's for sale today;
Now, sell it at the royal hall –
But for no other price at all
    Except a pair of eyes.'

Down in the gateway sat the lad;
    A golden bobbin now he had.
Out of the window the queen did peep:
"Oh, if that cone were mine to keep,
    to match this distaff too!"

"Go again, mother, ask for me
    What that bobbin's price might be?"
'Eyes, my lady,' said the lad,
'That's the order from my dad:
    Nothing but two eyes.'

"Eyes? That's a price that's new to me!
    And who, boy, might your father be?"
'My father you don't need to know;
who looks for him won't find him so;
    he comes by himself.'

46   The Golden Spinning-wheel

"Mother, dear mother, what's to pay?
But I must have that cone today!
Go to my chamber, up the stair;
Our Dora's eyes are hidden there.
    Let him take them now."

The youngster took the eyes, and then
Back to the woods he ran again.
'Lad, bring the living-water charm,
to make this body free from harm
    just as it was before.'

Eyes in their sockets he did fit;
The flame, once quenched, again was lit;
The girl awoke, looked all around –
But nobody at all she found,
    Only herself alone.

V

Joyfully, when three weeks had gone,
The king returned – the war was won.
'My own dear lady, how are you?
Did you remember what to do
    From my parting words?'

"To heart I took them, as I ought,
    and look – just see what I have bought!
This spinning-wheel's unique, I'm sure –
Distaff and bobbin – gold, all pure!
    All out of love for you!"

'Come here, my lady; sit down, see,
    spin golden thread for love of me.'
Down at the wheel she blithely sat –
Grew pale and trembled – look at that!
    Oh dear, what a song!

"Whirr – an evil thread you spin!
    You came here to deceive the king:
Your own stepsister you did slay,
And tore her limbs and eyes away –
    Whirr – an evil thread!"

'What kind of wheel have you got there?
    And what's that song? A strange affair!
Play it again for me, my dear –
What the words mean, I've no idea.
    Spin, my lady, spin!'

"Whirr – an evil thread you spin!
    You wanted to deceive the king:
His true fiancée you did slay
And cheated him, her part to play –
    Whirr – an evil thread!"

'A fearful song you play to me!
  You are not what you seem to be!
Play a third time for me, my dear,
That the whole message I may hear:
  Spin, my lady, spin!'

"Whirr – an evil thread you spin!
  You came here to deceive the king:
In the woods, in a rocky hole,
Your sister lies – her lord you stole!
  Whirr – an evil thread!"

The king heard all, and understood –
  Leapt on his horse, rode to the wood;
Calling, he searched the forests wide:
'Where are you, Dornička?' he cried.
  'Where are you, dearest love?'

VI

Around the woods, broad acres lie;
  With his true wife the lord rides by.
They ride a fiery jet-black steed,
Whose shoes ring merrily indeed,
  Back to the royal hall.

Again there came a wedding-day;
The virgin bride like flowers in May;
And there was merrymaking, feasting,
Music and dancing without ceasing,
   All for three whole weeks.

What of that mother, wicked witch?
What of that girl, snake-hearted bitch?
Four wolves came loping from the wood;
Each seized a woman by one foot,
   Gripping their bodies fast.

They tore the eyeballs from their heads,
And ripped their arms and legs to shreds.
What had been done to that poor maid
Was now the price those women paid,
   Down in the forest deep.

What of that golden spinning-wheel?
What might its song be now, what spiel?
Only for three times did it play;
No-one has heard it since that day,
   No more was it seen.

Christmas Eve

I

Dark as the grave; frost on the window glimmers,
    Warmth from the stove through the parlour spreads;
An old wife's dozing; on the hearth, fire shimmers;
    Girls are spinning soft flaxen thread.

'Spinning-wheel, spinning-wheel, whir around,
See, Advent soon will be coming round,
    And closer and closer comes Christmas Eve!

Gladly and freely the girls are spinning
    All through these gloomy winter eves;
Their work's not in vain, there's a prize for the winning,
    Every one firmly hopes and believes.

To the busy girl comes a young man duly,
    Saying, 'Come, my lass, come to me;
Be my wife, and I'll love you truly;
    A faithful husband to you I'll be.

You'll be my wife and I'll be your man –
    My dearest, give me your hand to take!'
And the maiden, who once such fine thread span,
    Now has the wedding shirts to make.

Spinning-wheel, spinning-wheel, whir around,
Advent soon will be coming round,
    And Christmas Eve is at the door!'

II

Hey there, feast of Christmas Eve,
    Full of mystery,
What good gift to each will you
    Bring in memory?

The landlord gets a Christmas loaf;
    Cows, scraps from our plates;
Garlic for the cockerel,
    Peas for all his mates.

To the fruit-tree, fish-bones left
    After supper fall;
And those who keep the fast will see
    Gold pigs on the wall.

Hey there, I'm a maiden young,
    Heart still uncommitted;
One boy, then another one
    Through my thoughts has flitted.

Beneath the woods, beneath the woods,
　　On the lord's estate,

Ancient willows stand, grey heads
　　Bowed beneath snow's weight.

One hunched willow's pointing down
　　Secretly to show
Where the lake's blue waters hide
　　Under ice and snow.

If girls, they say, at midnight go
　　By moonlight to that place,
The destined lad will show himself
　　Upon the water's face.

Ha, midnight doesn't frighten me,
　　Nor silly witches, too;
I'll go along and take an axe
　　To chop the ice right through.

And down I'll look into the lake,
　　As deep as deep can be,
And gaze upon my own true love,
　　Eye to eye, steadily.

III

Marie, Hana, two names so charming,
    Girls like spring roses, fresh and pure;
Which of the pair was the greater darling,
    No-one ever could tell for sure.

If to a lad one spoke for a while, then
    For her sake through a fire he'd go;
But if the second gave him a smile, then
    Out of his thoughts the first would blow!

Midnight had come. In the heavens so wide,
    A scatter of tiny stars was strewn,
Like little sheep round their shepherd-guide,
    For their shepherd, the clear bright moon.

Midnight had come, of all nights the mother,
    Midnight on holy Christmas Eve;
Straight to the lake, from one way and another,
    Fresh tracks in young snow were plain to perceive.

Her face to the water the first one bends;
    The second stands by as she drops to her knee:
'Golden heart, Hana, my dearest friend –
    what kind of vision there can you see?'

"I see a cottage – it's quite obscure, now,
  like Václav's home it seems to be –
it's getting clearer – yes, there's the door now –
  and in the door a man's form I see!

A dark green coat on his back he's wearing,
  I know him! – a hat with a tilted brim,
On it, the posy I gave as a fairing –
  Dear God in heaven! It's Václav! It's him!"

Her heart is thumping, she jumps to her feet,
  Beside her, the other drops to her knee:
"Good luck, my darling Marie, my sweet –
  What kind of vision can you see?"

'I see, I see – lots of mist, it's seeming,
  with that mist it's all dark as ink;
out of it there's a red light gleaming –
  it looks as if we're in church, I think.

A black shape's forming amid the whiteness –
  Now it's dawning, the light's come back: –
Bridesmaids there, and against their brightness –
  Heavens – a coffin – a cross of black!'

IV

Over ears of young green corn,
  Warm, soft breezes play;
Field and orchard, bright with flowers
  Wear their best array.
From the church, music leaps like flame one morning;
Then, with hurrahs, strewn with flowers for adorning
  A wedding rides away.

The bonny bridegroom's like a flower,
  Round him groomsmen ride;
Dark green coat, and jaunty hat
  Tilted to one side:
Just as she saw him in that hour of fate,
Now he is taking her home as his mate –
  Hana, his bonny bride.

* * *

Summer's gone. Across the fields
  Chilly winds are blowing.
Bells are tolling. With a corpse
  On a bier they're going:
Weeping and mourning, bridesmaids all in white,
Deep-voiced trumpets calling through the candlelight:
From the depths intoning:
  Miserere mei!

Whose is that wreath of evergreen,
 Whose coffin on the bier?
She is dead, ah, she is dead,
 Pure lily without peer!
She bloomed as if watered by dew, fresh and blithe;
Withered in death, as if felled by a scythe –
 Poor, ah, poor Marie!

V

Winter has come; frost on the window glimmers,
 Warmth from the stove through the parlour spreads;
The old wife's reclining; on the hearth, fire shimmers;
 Once more the girls are spinning thread.

'Spinning-wheel, spinning-wheel, whir around,
Once again Advent will soon come round,
 And Christmas Eve's not far away!

'Ah, you holy Christmas Eve,
 Night so rich in wonder!
When I think of you, sharp pain
 Splits my heart asunder.

'Just like this we sat last year,
    All of us together:
And, before the year was out,
    Two were gone forever!

'One, head in a kerchief wound,
    Little shirts sews here;
In black earth the other rots
    This last quarter-year –
    Poor, ah, poor Marie!

'As we sat then, we shall sit
    Tomorrow, and today:
And, before the year is out,
    Who will go which way?

'Spinning-wheel, spinning-wheel, whir around,
All in the world goes round and round,
    And human life is like a dream!

'Better to dream on in hope mistaken,
    Darkness before us, with nothing to see,
Than discover the future, and to awaken
    Knowing its terrible certainty!'

For Katharine, b. 24. 12. 1982.

The Wild Dove

All around the churchyard
  Goes a winding way;
There a widow young and fair
  Weeping, walked one day.

For the husband she had lost
  She wept and sorrowed,
As for the final time
  After him she followed.

From the white-walled courtyard,
  Over the green meadow,
With a feather in his hat
  Rides a smart young fellow.

'Do not weep, do not cry,
it'll spoil your eyes;
Young and pretty widow,
Hear a word that's wise.

'Do not weep, do not cry,
if your husband's dead –
charming widow, pretty rose,
marry me instead.'

One more day, still she wept;
The next in silence passed,
Then, on the third, her grief
Slowly died at last.

That day, from her thoughts
The dead man she was shaking,
And, before the month was out,
Her wedding-dress was making.

A merrier procession
Round the churchyard rides;
Driving this way, driving
A bridegroom and his bride.

A wedding, yes, a wedding
Full of noise and cheer:
In her new husband's arms
See the bride appear.

A wedding, yes, a wedding –
Music played so sweetly;
He pressed her close to him,
She just laughed discreetly.

Laugh, bride, laugh, it suits you –
What a charming sound!
Deaf ears has that dead man
Underneath the ground!

Clasp him, your beloved –
You don't need to fear;
It's tight enough, that coffin –
He won't come back here!

Kiss him, ah yes, kiss him –
Longed-for face, young wife;
The man you mixed that potion
Won't come back to life!

* * *

Time is flying, flying,
Nothing's as before;
What was not, is coming,
What was, is no more.

Time is flying, flying;
Hours, years, have their term;
One thing never changes:
Guilt alone stands firm.

Three years he's been lying,
The dead man, in his grave;
On the mound that marks it
Fresh green grasses wave.

On the mound, grasses;
At his head, a young oak grows;
On that young oak-tree sits
A small dove, white as snow.

There it sits, there it sits
With its plaintive coo;
Everyone who hears it feels
His heart will break in two.

One woman, most of all,
Feels hers break this way;
From her head she tears the hair,
Calling in dismay:

'Do not hoot, do not call,
Dinning in my ears;
That cruel song of yours
Through my soul does pierce!

Do not hoot, don't accuse;
My head is spinning round:
Or hoot to make it fly
In pieces at a bound!'

Water's flowing, flowing,
Wave on wave is surging,
See there, among the waves,
A white dress emerging.

Here a foot goes floating by,
There a pale hand waves;
That woman, poor lost soul,
Goes to seek her grave!

They pulled her to the bank,
Secretly to lie
Buried where footpaths cross
In a field of rye.

She had no tomb at all
As her last abode;
Only a massive stone
Pressed her with its load.

Never, though, could any stone
Lie upon her frame,
Heavy as the curse whose weight
Rests upon her name!

Záhoř's Bed

I

    Over the forests, mists are flowing grey,
Like ghostly forms in procession drifting by;
To another country the crane flies away –
Bleak and unwelcoming fields and orchards lie.
Out of the west the wind is blowing chill,
And yellowed leaves are singing a song soft and still.
Well-known is that song; for every autumn season
Leaves upon the oak-tree whisper it anew:
Yet those who understand its words are but few,
And he who understands, to smile has no reason.

    Unknown pilgrim in your sombre habit, say,
With that long staff in your hand, and that rosary,
And the cross upon your staff – who might you be,
Where are you going to so late in the day?
Where are you hurrying? Your feet are bare,
Autumn is chilly, and cold dew lies there:
Stay here with us, for good people are we,
Everyone's happy a good guest to see.

Ah, you dear pilgrim – as yet you're only young,
And no beard as yet to hide your chin has sprung,
Your cheek's just like that of a pretty maiden –
But how pale and sadly faded and shrunken,
Deep in their sockets, too, your eyes are sunken!
Is your heart perhaps with secret sorrow laden?
Does unhappiness on your body prey?
Pressing it earthwards with the years so grey?

Handsome young man, don't go into the night;
We'd gladly help you, if only we might,
Maybe at least some aid we could provide.
Come, don't pass by; rest that body of yours:
There is no grief that no remedy cures,
Potent balsam rests in the trust to confide. –

Not once he lifts his eyes – unhearing, unaware;
Out of his dreaming there's no way to draw him!
On now he makes his way through the brushwood there:
God give him strength for the pilgrimage before him!

II

Fields stretching far away, fields stretching wide,
Long, long the path running over fields and lands;
There on a mound a slender spar there stands,
Topping that hillock at the pathway's side.
Not a single branch has that slender fir-tree,
Only, fixed across its top, a small piece of board,
And on that cross-piece, nailed for all to see,
A rain-blurred image of Christ our Lord.
Down towards the right his bloodstained head droops low,
Hands pierced through and through he stretches out so wide:
Two sides of the world he points with them to show,
How the road is leading to two opposite sides:
His right towards the east, the birthplace of light,
His left towards the west, whose overlord is night.
There to the east is the portal of heaven,
In paradise eternal God's own saints abide;
And all who do good the certain hope are given
That they too will share the rejoicing at their side.
But to the west the infernal gates stand:
Brimstone and pitch in an ocean are burning;
There are the devils, an accursed, evil band,
The souls of the damned on fiery wheels turning.
Grant that your children may reach the right, Lord Jesus –
But from the kingdom on the left release us!

There on that mound, as dawn's first light is shining,
At break of day, our youthful pilgrim's kneeling,
Tight round the cross his arms he is entwining,
Warmly embracing that wood without feeling.
Whispering now, as tears run from his eye,
Now again heaving a deep, heavy sigh.

Just so, when parting from his beloved girl,
Some young man in love bestows a final greeting,
Travelling away to strange parts of the world,
With no certain knowledge of another meeting:
Yet another final passionate embrace,
Yet another kiss like a burning flame – one more:
Now fare you well, you darling girl whom I adore:
Ill-starred is the hour that drives me from this place!

Face as white as chalk, icily he gazes,
But in his heart a fierce, wild flame is burning;
Suddenly the pilgrim from the ground his body raises,
And to the west his rapid steps is turning.

Shortly he vanishes among the wood's thick boughs:
May God succour him on his journey now!

III

There stands, there stands a rock, in the forest deep,
Past it through hawthorn bushes winds the way,
And on that rock a gigantic oak rears steep,
Over eternal wilderness that age-old king holds sway.
Heavenwards it cranes a brow all bare and stark,
Green arms it is holding out on every side;
Tough bark coat by lightning ploughed with furrows wide,
Rotten is its body under the bark:
A most convenient hollow, room enough to spare –
For some savage forest beast a cosy lair!

Look! On a mossy bed, beneath that oak-tree there,
Whose can that enormous, fearful figure be?
Animal or man in the pelt of a bear?
Scarcely in that shape a human could one see!
His body is a rock, lying on the rock up there,
His limbs the knotted muscles of the oak-trunk's boughs,
Flowing into one are his beard and his hair,
Sootily shadowed is his face by bristling brows;
Under his brows a penetrating stare,
Poisonous his gaze is, just like the eyes
Gazing from the green grass where a serpent lies.
Who is this man? And that sombre, brooding brow –
What are the cunning schemes that keep it clouded now?
Who is this man? What does he want, in a place so bleak?

Ask me no questions! In the thickets seek
On both sides of the path; ask those bones instead,
Over there decaying, in the dust laid low;
Ask those black unfriendly guests, who, overhead,
Fly round in circles, croaking as they go:
Many things they have seen – and still more they know!

But the forest man is leaping from his bed,
Fixed on the pathway, fiercely burns his gaze;
Whirling a monstrous cudgel round his head,
Down the path he bounds, and in its centre stays.

Who comes this way? – A youth in a habit is he,
A cross in his hand, at his waist a rosary! –
Take flight, young man! And turn back, as you ought!
Your journey's leading you to certain death and sure.
Even without this, human life is short,
And what a waste of your youth, unspoilt and pure!
Turn around and take flight, while strength enough remains,
To where no monstrous club waits to dash out your brains!
And to smash in pieces your head, still so tender! –

Nothing does he see or hear; sunk deep in his woes,
Further still, with measured steps, straight ahead he goes,
On to that place where his life he must surrender.

'Stop, worm! Who are you? And which way leads your trail?'

Halting, the pilgrim lifts up his face so pale:
"I am an outcast," he quietly replies.
"On to Satan's kingdom, to hell my pathway lies!"

'Ho, ho – to hell, then? In all these forty years,
many things I've come to hear, many things to see,
but a song like that, while I've been sitting here,
nobody till now has ever sung to me!
Not a step you'll need to take, nor to breathe a sigh,
I'll transport you there myself – ho, ho! to hell?
But when my score of years is full, by and by,
I might come after you for breakfast there as well!'

"Do not blaspheme against the grace of Our Lord!
Even before I beheld my life's first day,
To hell in my father's blood I was signed away,
Bartered for earthly goods – by a devil's fraud.
Great is God's mercy! and the holy cross's spell
Even can break the dreadful bars of hell.
It can conquer Satan with all his powers and might!
Great is God's mercy! to grant this boon it yearns,
That the feeble pilgrim a victor may return,
Wresting the document from infernal night."

'What do you mean? In all these forty years,
Men without number off to hell I've packed,
But none of them as yet has made the journey back!
Your complexion's young and soft – worm, listen here!
You'd be good today, instead of these tough beasts,

As a little tit-bit before my evening feast:
But I'll set you free – I will let you go –
Yet no-one at all, of those who came this way,
Ever from my knotted cudgel got away!
Worm, I'll release you! But this I want to know:
Promise that afterwards faithfully you'll tell
What you have seen, and what you have learnt in hell.'

   Down stooped the pilgrim, and lifted up on high
His pilgrim staff, surmounted with the cross's sign:
"By the glory of this holy cross I swear
that a true report from hell to you I'll bear!"

IV

Winter is over; snows on the mountains thaw,
In the valleys flood-waters swell with snow and rain;
Home from far countries the crane returns once more:
Our pilgrim, though, has not yet arrived again.

Green in the forest, twigs are clad in glory,
The violet beneath the flint breathes its lovely smell,
Nightingale there is telling his long story,
But no tidings come from the kingdom of hell.

Spring is past, and summer; short the days now grow,
Chill the air is turning, as leaves fall and fall;
But no tidings come from hell – no, none at all.
Might the pilgrim still return yet, even so?
Has his body fallen on the way, collapsed?
Or has hell engulfed him in its maw, perhaps?

Beneath the oak on high, the forest man stands there,
Face turned towards the west, gloomily he stares;
Grumbling, he sits there: 'Of those who came this way,
From my knotted cudgel no-one got away!
Only one man to keep his word I bound,
that was the only one – and he let me down!'

"I did not let you down!" declares, with haughty pride,
the voice of the pilgrim that moment at his side;
upright is his figure, eyes severe and bold,
and on his brow tranquillity lies cold.
And from that pale and noble face of his, it seemed
As if the sunlight's clear blazing radiance streamed.

"By the oath I swore – I did not let you down! –
fast to you, God's sinful servant, I am bound;
and now once more I swear this vow to you I make:
By the glory of this holy cross I swear
That a true report from hell to you I bear!"

Hearing these words, the forest man began to shake,
Grasping for his weapon, to his feet he bounded:
But as struck by lightning, there he stood astounded –
For his eyes the gaze of the pilgrim could not take.

"Sit there and listen! Stories grim to tell
I'm bringing back to you from my trip to hell:
Testimony of God's wrath my words can show:
Infinitely greater is God's mercy, though!"
What he saw in hell the pilgrim did report:
An ocean of flames – the devils' loathsome crew;
And how life with death everlasting did consort
In eternal torments for the damned, ever new.

Scowling, the forest man sat underneath the oak,
Staring straight before him – not a word he spoke.

What he heard in hell the pilgrim did report:
Piteous lamentation – the damned who cursed and swore –
Crying aloud for help – but nobody he saw
Who might come to help them, or offer them support,
Just a curse eternal, damnation evermore! –

Scowling, the forest man sat underneath the oak,
Staring straight before him – not a word he spoke.

Then the pilgrim told him how Satan, prince of hell,
By the holy cross's sign he did compel
To command the devil who planned that wicked fraud
That he should return the parchment signed in blood.
Stubbornly the devil the infernal lord withstood,
And defied his orders – the bond was not restored.

Satan was enraged, and commanded in his wrath:
'Go now and bathe him in the infernal bath!'
To fulfil his orders a troop of demons came;
They prepared a bath all out of ice and flame:
On the one side fire like burning coal was blazing,
On the other, frost over icy stone was glazing;
And, when they saw the measure filled, then in a trice
Back to flame the troop transformed the mass of ice.
Terribly the devil roared, writhing like a snake,
Till it seemed his heart and mind were about to break.
Then Satan gave a sign; away went all the pack,
And new strength again to the devil flooded back.
But when, released, he could freely breathe once more,
That parchment signed in blood he refused to restore.

Satan was enraged, and in his fury yelled:
'Now in his arms the infernal maiden must be held!'
This was a maiden formed of iron cold,
Arms stretching out to the love for whom she yearned,
Close to her cruel breast the devil she did fold,
Squeezing till all his bones were crushed and churned.
Terribly the devil roared, writhing like a snake,
Till it seemed his heart and mind were about to break.
Then Satan gave a sign; the maiden's grip grew slack
And new strength again to the devil flooded back.
But when, released, he could freely breathe once more,
That parchment signed in blood he refused to restore.

Then Satan roared aloud the final words he said:
'Take him and throw him upon Záhoř's bed!'

'On the bed of Záhoř? – what's that? – on Záhoř's bed?' –
the strange forest man cries out in agony,
his monstrous body trembling like an aspen tree,
sweat bursting forth from the tough skin of his head.
'On the bed of Záhoř! – Záhoř is the name
once my mother often used to speak – just the same,
when she was teaching me mats to weave and thread,
when with those mats on moss a bed for me she made
and, as a cover, a wolfskin on me laid.
And now in hell is the place of Záhoř's bed – ?
Come you – you servant of God, quickly tell,
What's waiting there for Záhoř on that bed in hell?'

"Righteous is God's hand of vengeance, just and sure,
but forever hidden from us his judgments stay:
I know not the torments in hell you must endure,
But not a whit less than all your crimes are they.
Know this, though – the devil, hearing those words said,
Threatened with the punishment of Záhoř's own bed,
Gave back the blood-signed note without delay!"

A pine on the hillside has stood a century,
Proudly to heaven stretching up its crown:
Then comes an axe; as it bows its head, the tree
Heavily falling, to earth sinks shuddering down.

The wild forest aurochs in his strength's abundant prime
In the forest wrenches from their roots the mighty trees:
Pierced by a javelin, he staggers for a time,
Then falls, bellowing in mortal agonies.

So did the forest man. Crushed by these tidings,
Down to earth he sinks in mortal terror's grasp;
Beats his club against his head, roaring and writhing,
And, rolling in the dust, the pilgrim's feet he clasps:
'Help me, oh, man of God, help – oh, pity me!
Let not that bed in hell be my destiny!'

"Do not say such things to me! I'm a worm, like you,
if God's grace did not prevail, lost for evermore:
to it you must turn, and from that must seek a cure,
While the right time's yet at hand, penance you must do."

'How should I repent? Upon my staff here – see
these rows of notches, many as they be –
count them if you can – yes, every single one,
each of those notches marks a murder I've done!'

Earthwards stoops the pilgrim; high aloft swings he
Záhoř's club – the trunk of a mighty apple-tree –
Thrusting it into the hard rock's summit now,
Just like a slender twig in earth fresh from the plough.

"There, before the witness of your fell deeds, I say –
kneel, cruel ruffian – kneel by night and day!
Do not reckon time; ignore hunger – thirst, as well –
The tally of your crimes is all you must tell,
Pray to God – beseech Him to wipe your guilt away.
Great your guilt is – heavy too, with no parallel:
Though unparalleled be the penance you must do,
There is no limit to God's compassion too!
Kneel there and wait for me – until, in a space,
I may return again to you through God's own grace."

Thus speaks the pilgrim, and goes upon his way. –
Záhoř is kneeling, and kneeling he does stay;
He neither eats nor drinks, kneeling day and night;
God's mercy he implores, praying with deep sighs –
Day follows after day; fast the snow now flies.
Now, too, the frosts come on with their icy bite.
Záhoř kneels on, and from prayer does not refrain –
But for the pilgrim he waits and waits in vain,
He never comes to him, back from where he went –
May God be merciful to the penitent!

V

Now across the world have flown fourscore years and ten;
In the days between many a change has come around:
The one who, at that time, was but an infant then
Now is an old man, and for the grave he's bound.
Very few, though, have survived to see this day;
All the rest in the grave are hidden away.
Another generation – all its faces strange –
All the world is altered, wherever man might range:
Only the sun up there, in the heavens blue,
In that alone not the slightest change you'll find;
And, as through the ages it has gladdened mankind,
Nowadays as ever it brings joy to you!

Spring's here again. A warm, soft breeze is playing,
The nightingale again has his stories to tell;
Fresh in the meadows, grass is rocking, swaying,
And once more the violet gives out its sweet new smell.

Through the deep woods, shaded by the hawthorn's bough,
Down the path two pilgrims are making their way:
With a staff in his hand, an old man bent and bowed –
With a bishop's staff – with age he's trembling now,
At his side a handsome youth, acting as his stay.

"Wait a while, my son! For a little rest I crave –
ah, now my spirit is longing for repose!
Would I were gathered to my fathers in the grave!
God's mercy, though, has other tasks on me to impose.
Great is God's mercy! For through the gates of hell
By its mighty power His servant it did bring;
To His holy office it raised him up, as well,
And therefore my soul magnifies its Lord and King.
Firmly to you, Lord, my hope I did confide:
Grant that on earth your glory may abide! –
Son of mine, I'm thirsty! Look around and see:
I feel, unless my fainting senses deceive me,
Close by you will find refreshment to relieve me,
That my life's task may be accomplished finally."

Off went the young man along the forest's side,
Seeking to find a place where a spring might hide.
Far he strides, farther still, breaking through the bushes,
Till through to the mossy rock his way he pushes.
Suddenly, though, his foot stops abruptly there;
And, just like a glow-worm that through the twilight flies,
Over his handsome face there flickers bright surprise:
Strangely an unknown scent comes drifting through the air,
A scent of endless sweetness no words could describe,
As if in Paradise's orchards he'd arrived.
And, when the young man through thick brushwood there
Squeezes his way upwards, and on the rock alights,
What should his eyes behold but a matchless sight?
Bushy-leaved, a tree stands on the rock so bare:
It is an apple-tree; wide its branches range,

And on it are ripening fruits of beauty strange –
Apples of gold – and from them comes wafting out
That scent of Paradise through all the woods about.

    In the young man's body his heart leapt high with glee,
Setting his lively glance sparkling merrily:
'Ah, surely, surely gracious God did make
wonders and miracles for the old man's sake:
Instead of cold water, this succour he supplies –
Bleak rock in the forest bears fruits of Paradise.'

    But as with pleasure he was stretching out his arm,
Reaching for the apple, he drew back in alarm.

    "Leave it, don't pick it – you did not plant that tree!"
Tersely a voice, deep and hollow, did command,
Close the voice was – coming from the ground, seemingly,
Yet, all around, he saw no-one else at hand.
Only one great tree-stump standing by his side,
Covered with blackberries intertwined with moss,
And fragments of an ancient oak-tree, besides,
Its bole with a gaping hollow split across.

    Round the trunk the young man walked; at the hole he stares,
Walked round all the landscape that lies about it there;
Not a trace of footprints, though, can he detect,
Showing him where a human foot might have stepped,
Just empty wilderness he sees everywhere.

'Maybe my ear was tricked – leading me astray?
Maybe some wild animal roared far away?
Could water in the rock have made that sound, maybe?'
Said the young man to himself; the sound he ignored,
And for the apple stretched out his hand once more.

"Leave it, don't pick it – you did not plant that tree!"
Thundering still louder, forbids that voice so hollow.
Then, as the youth looks round, the voice to follow –
See! The great tree-stump, amid the twists of bramble,
Starts to move – then, from among the mosses shamble
Two long arms, pointing towards the young man, turning –
And above the arms, like pitch-candles, burning
On a foggy night, two eyes of red, glaring,
Under the mosses grey roll towards him, staring.

Overcome, the young man, in terror and dismay,
Signs himself with holy crosses – one, two and three;
And, like a hawk who from its nest is scared away,
Never seeks the path, sees no barriers in his way,
Straight down the rock through the undergrowth he flees;
Spattered with blood from the sharp twigs of the trees,
Falls to the ground close to where the old man lay.

'Master, oh, master! There's evil in this wood:
there on that flat-topped rock an apple-tree grows thick,
bearing ripe fruits in springtime there it stood –
and a great tree-stump prevents those who would pick.
And that same tree-stump has rolling eyes, and talks –
Grabs with an arm those who to the tree might walk:
oh, master, this is the kingdom of Old Nick!'

"You are wrong, son of mine! This is God's own grace,
working his miracles – to him glory be!
Now that my pilgrimage is ending, as I see,
gladly would my body lie here in earth's embrace.
Now, my son, do me a service one last time!
Take me up that flat-topped rock – help me to climb."

So the young man did; and across the brushwood there,
Lying in their path, the old man he had to bear.

Upwards now towards the apple-tree they go –
Look! Before the old man the tree-stump bows low,
Stretching out its arms to him, joyfully crowing:
'Master, ah! my master! You took so long – but see:
there on that seedling of yours now fruit is growing –
ah, master, pick it – for you did plant that tree!'

"Záhoř, o Záhoř! May peace now come upon you:
Peace I bring that in my last days I have won you!
Boundless is God's mercy, endless, we can tell –
Both of us it snatched away from that bed in hell!
Grant me that release which I to you have given:
Let our ashes rest here, side by side, where they fell,
And our souls be taken by angels from heaven!"

'Amen!' said Záhoř – and that minute, then and there,
crumbled to dust, in a modest little heap;
all that was left of him on the stone so bare
was a twist of brambles, his memory to keep.

Dead to earth that instant the old man too dropped prone.
His earthly pilgrimage is over now, fulfilled!
In the middle of the woods the youth remained alone,
Till he should have carried out what his master willed.

But that same moment, above his head in flight,
Hovering there came two doves of purest white;
Hovering in joyful dance higher and higher,
Till up they soared at last to the angels' choir.

The Water-goblin

I

On a poplar by the pool
The Goblin sat at twilight cool:
    'Glow, moon, glow,
    That my thread may sew.

'For myself new boots I'm sewing,
On dry land and water going:
    Glow, moon, glow,
    That my thread may sew.

'Thursday now – tomorrow's Friday –
sew a coat all trim and tidy:
    Glow, moon, glow,
    That my thread may sew.

'Coat of green and boots of red,
For tomorrow I'll be wed:
    Glow, moon, glow,
    That my thread may sew.'

II

At first light a young girl rose,
In a bundle tied her clothes:
    'I'll go, mother, to the lake;
    all my things to wash I'll take.'

"Don't go, don't go to the water,
stay at home today, my daughter!
    In the night I dreamed bad dreams:
    Don't go, daughter, where it streams.

"First a string of pearls I chose you,
Then in robes of white I clothed you,
    Skirts that swirled like foaming water:
    Don't go to the lake, my daughter.

"Grief's concealed in that white dress,
Pearls hide tears of deep distress,
    Friday's an unlucky day,
    Don't go, daughter – keep away!"

But the daughter cannot rest;
To the lake, as if possessed,
    To the lake, as if pursued –
    Home no longer suits her mood.

As the first dress she was soaking,
Under her the bridge fell broken,
    And upon that poor young girl
    Closed the eddying water's whirl.

From the depths great waves came rolling,
Ripples in wide rings unfolding;
    On the rock by the poplar tree,
    A small green figure clapped with glee.

III

Gloomy are those watery realms,
Desolate are they;
    Water-lilies float above
    Grass where fishes play.

There no sunlight spreads its warmth,
No breeze stirs the air;
    Cold and silent, like a heart
    Hopeless with despair.

Gloomy are those watery realms,
Desolate are they;
    Half in darkness, half in light
    Day glides after day.

Spacious are the Goblin's courts,
Of wealth he has his fill;
    But the guests who visit them
    Stay against their will.

If beyond their crystal gates
A traveller should explore,
    Rarely will his loved ones' eyes
    Ever see him more.

Between the gates the Goblin sits,
Fishing-nets he's mending;
    While his young wife by his side
    Her new baby's tending.

'Rockabye, my little son,
born to one unwilling,
    While you're smiling up at me,
    Grief my heart is killing.

'Happily you stretch to me
Little hands, and wave;
    Up on earth I'd rather be,
    Lying in my grave.

'In the earth, beside the church
With a black cross near –
    Then at least she'd have me close,
    My poor mother dear.

'Rockabye, my little son,
Tiny goblin-lad;
    How, when I remember her,
    Can I not grow sad?

'Anxiously she used to plan
To what man she'd give me;
    Never once did she expect
    That she might outlive me!

'I got married, yes indeed,
But against her wishes;
    Crayfish black the groomsmen were,
    And the bridesmaids – fishes!

'And my man – God pity me!
– on dry land walks seeping;
    in the water, under jars
    human souls he's keeping.

'Rockabye, my little son,
With your moss-green hair;
    Mother's wedding didn't bring her
    Home to loving care.

'In a web of cunning nets
Tangled and beguiled,
    Here she has no happiness,
    Only you, my child!'

"What's that song of yours, my wife?
I don't like your singing!
    Songs like that pierce heart and mind,
    Bitter anger bringing.

"Stop your song at once, my wife,
gall within me swells:
    Many girls I've turned to fish –
    You'll be one as well!"

'Don't be angry, don't be cross,
Goblin, husband dear!
    Do not blame a faded rose,
    Crushed and withered here.

'Like a tree in spring, my youth
you have snapped and broken;
    yet no kindness for my sake
    have you done or spoken.

'I've begged you a hundred times –
sweetly I'd implore:
    let me go to mother once,
    just one short time more.

'I've begged you a hundred times –
floods of tears I'd cry –
    let me see her once again
    for a last goodbye!

'I've begged you a hundred times –
On my knees I'd fall;
    But the hard rind of your heart
    Softened not at all!

'Don't be angry, don't be cross,
Goblin dear, my master!
    If you must, then let your wrath
    Make my doom come faster.

'If you'd turn me to a fish
So that dumb I'd be,
    Rather change me to a stone
    With no memory.

'Rather change me to a stone
With no thought or feeling:
    So I'd never grieve again
    For the sun's bright wheeling!'

"If I could believe your words,
happy, wife, I'd be;
    but who can catch the same fish twice
    in the open sea?

"Neither would I hold you back
From visiting your mother;
    But women's empty thoughts, I fear,
    Are one thing – deeds another!

"Well, then – I will let you go,
From my kingdom's borders;
    But command that faithfully
    You must obey my orders.

"Don't take your mother in your arms,
Nor any other soul
    Lest that earthly love of yours
    Finds an unearthly goal.

"From dawn to dusk, no-one at all
in your arms you must take;
    and when the vesper bells ring out,
    come back to the lake.

"From morning bell to evening bell
You can go – that may be;
    One condition: as a pledge
    You must leave the baby."

IV

What would early summer be like
    If it lacked the sun's bright face?
What would a reunion be like
    If it lacked a warm embrace?

And if a child, so long apart,
 Clasps her mother to her heart,
Who could blame a loving daughter
   For that act in such a case?

All day they console each other,
   Though their tears fall like a shower.
'Goodbye now, my darling mother –
   oh, I fear the evening hour!'
"Don't be frightened, daughter dear;
of that devil have no fear;
I'll make sure that water-monster
   Never gets you in his power!"

Evening's come. Outside, the green man
   Stalks about within the yard.
In their room, the girl and mother
   Crouch, the door tight-wedged and barred.
"Don't be frightened, daughter dear;
nothing's going to harm you here;
the devil from the lake is powerless
   up on land that's dry and hard."

When the vesper bells were ringing,
   Bang! – a knock the door did shake.
"Come along, my wife, come home now,
   supper-time – there's food to make!"
"Crafty devil, get away
from our threshold – go, I say!
What you used to have for supper –
Go and eat it in the lake!"

Bang! – the splintered door at midnight
 Shook with knocks to wake the dead:
"Come along, my wife, come home now,
 for you have to make my bed."
'Crafty devil, get away
From our threshold – go, I say!
Let whoever used to make it
 Come and do the job instead!'

Bang! A third time came the knocking
 As the morning light grew grey:
"Come along, my wife, come home now,
 Baby's crying for milk, I say!" –
'Mother, agony past bearing
for my child my heart is tearing!
Mother mine, oh, dearest mother,
 let me, let me go away!'

"No, my girl – you're going nowhere!
 That fiend's plotting something new;
If you're worried for your baby,
 Greater is my fear for you.
Get back, murderer, to the water!
I won't let you take my daughter:
If your little one is crying,
 Bring it to our threshold – do!"

On the lake the storm is shrieking;
    In the storm the child screams shrill;
Screams that pierce the soul with anguish,
    Then they suddenly fall still.
'Oh, my mother, please, oh, please!
At those cries my blood will freeze –
Mother mine, oh, dearest mother,
    Fear of him my heart does fill!'

Something fell – beneath the doorway
    Moisture trickles – tinged with red.
When the old one went to open,
    What she saw filled her with dread.
In their blood, two objects lying
Sent cold terror through her flying:
Baby's head – without a body;
    Tiny body – with no head.

The Willow Tree

Early, at their morning meal,
To his young wife he appeals:

'Wife of mine, my lady dear,
you have always been sincere.

'Though you've always been sincere,
One thing you won't let me hear.

'Two years now we've been a couple –
Just one thing my mind does trouble.

'Dearest wife, my lady sweet,
What's the matter with your sleep?

'Strong and well you go to bed;
All night your body lies like dead.

'Not a movement, not a sound –
No trace of your soul is found.

'Cold your body grows, and colder
As if it in the grave did moulder.

'Even our baby's bitter crying
Will not wake you where you're lying.

'Golden lady, dearest wife,
Does some illness blight your life?

'If some illness should affect you,
Let some wise advice protect you.

'Many herbs grow in the field; you
Might, perhaps, find one that healed you.

'If herbs' strength is unavailing,
Words of power are all-prevailing.

'Words of power can clouds dispel,
Save ships when wild tempests swell.

'Words of power can quench a flame,
Crush a rock, and dragons tame.

'From the sky a bright star draw;
Such a word might bring a cure.'

"Dearest lord, my husband kind,
 don't let vain thoughts rack your mind.

"What the Fates at birth decree
 – for that there's no remedy.

"What Fate has appointed, too,
Human words cannot undo.

"In bed resting lifeless, I
Safely in God's power lie.

"Always safe beneath God's might;
He protects me every night.

"Though like the dead I sleep at night,
My soul returns with morning's light.

"I rise each morning, well and fit;
That's how God has ordered it!" –

Wife, your words are vain; your man's
Nurturing quite different plans.

By the fire an old crone squats,
And water pours from pot to pot.

In a row there stand twelve basins;
For advice to her he hastens.

'Mother, much you know and see,
Know each person's destiny.

'Where disease a victim's stalking,
Which way Death herself is walking.

'If you will, explain to me
What can my wife's problem be?

'Strong and well she goes to bed;
All night her body lies like dead.

'Not a movement, not a sound;
No trace of her soul is found.

'Cold her body grows, and colder,
As if it in the grave did moulder.'

"How can she not be dead, your wife,
since she has just half a life?

"At home with you while it is light,
Her soul lives in a tree at night.

"Go to the stream within the park;
You'll find a willow, white of bark;

"There a yellow bough is growing:
That's where your wife's soul is going!"

'I never wished to take a wife
who with a willow spent her life;

'With me my wife shall spend her days,
While that tree in the earth decays.'

On his shoulder he takes an axe;
The willow from its roots he hacks.

Into the stream its dead weight fell –
and from the depths, a rustling swelled.

It was rustling, it was sighing,
Like a mother who was dying.

Like a mother who, as she dies,
On her baby casts her eyes.

'What's that crowd around my door?
The death-knell's tolling – who's that for?'

"She is dead, the wife you cherished;
felled as by a scythe, she perished;

"brisk about her work, till she
tumbled like a falling tree;

"as she died, she breathed deep sighs,
and on her baby cast her eyes."

'Woe is me – oh, deepest woe!
I killed my wife – I could not know.

'And in that hour, that very one,
Orphaned him – our little son!

'Willow white, oh, willow tree,
What is this you've done to me?

'Half my life is gone with you;
In return, what shall I do?'

"From the water draw me now;
cut away my yellow bough;

"into planks then saw the stem;
have a cradle made from them.

"Let the baby in it lie,
So the poor mite shall not cry.

"With the rocking crib to hold him,
Mother's care will still enfold him.

"Plant the bough beside the river,
So no harm shall hurt it ever.

"When the little boy is grown,
He'll carve whistles of his own;

"Piping on those whistles gaily,
With his mother he'll talk daily."

The Lily

There died a maiden in life's springtime days,
As when a young rose withers and decays;
She died, that maiden, like a budding rose –
Ah, what a shame that in earth she should repose!

'Don't lay me in the village graveyard; there
Orphans' and widows' cries hang in the air;
There, too, so many bitter tears would flow
That my poor heart would break for very woe.

'Bury me rather in the woods so green,
Where on my grave the heather will be seen;
There little birds will sing their songs to me,
And my poor heart will dance for very glee.'

There had not passed a twelvemonth and a day,
When on her grave small heather-bells grew gay;
Nor had she lain three years beneath the ground,
When on her grave a flower so rare was found.

One pure white lily – if it you should see,
Sorrow would seize your heart mysteriously.
One fragrant lily – if you breathed its scent,
Right through your soul a flame of longing went.

"Hey, my companions, saddle up my black!
I'd go a-hunting down the greenwood track;
I'd go a-hunting under fir and pine;
It seems today that rare hunting will be mine!"

Halloo-ho – halloo! Loud his hounds do bay;
Hop! Neither ditch nor fence can bar his way.
Over the wicket-gate black and rider go –
Like an arrow in his path flies a white doe.

"Halloo-ho, halloo! Ha, my quarry rare,
 neither field nor thicket now your life can spare!"
Raising his arm, the lord prepares to smite –
There, in the doe's place, stands a lily white.

Wonderstruck, the lord on the lily gazed,
Arm all a-tremble, breathlessly amazed;
Thinking and thinking – high his chest did swell;
Was it the scent, or longing? Who could tell?

"Hey, faithful servant, set about your task:
 Dig up that lily – that is all I ask;
I wish that in my garden it should be –
Without it I can't live, it seems to me!

"Hey, faithful servant, trusty friend and true,
 Guard well that lily – watch it closely, too;
Carefully guard it for me day and night –
To it there draws me some strange and wondrous might!"

One day, then two days, he guarded it with care;
Great was the lord's joy in its grace so rare;
But on the third, as the full moon shed its light,
Off sped the servant to wake his lord by night.

"Get up, my master – there's no time to spare:
Your lily's trailing round the garden there;
Now is the moment – hurry, don't delay:
Your lily has a voice – strange things it does say!"

'Sadly at life's gate I drag out my days,
like dew upon the field, or misty river-haze;
When the first rays of sunlight brightly shine,
Perish dew, vapour, and this life of mine!'

"Your life won't perish – that I can assure,
and from the sun I'll give protection sure.
Stout walls to you will bring security,
And, dearest soul, my own wife you shall be."

So they were wed; she lived in blissful joy,
And to her husband she bore a little boy.
Sure of his happiness, the lord his hunt does praise;
Then a royal courier a note to him conveys.

'My faithful friend,' (thus wrote the king's own hand),
'Tomorrow at my service you must stand;
Let each loyal chieftain come at my desire,
All must leave home, as great need does require.'

Sadly to his dear wife he said goodbye,
As if he sensed ill-fortune was close by;
"If I myself your guardian cannot be,
 Mother I'll leave to guard you watchfully."

Badly his mother carried out his will,
Badly her task as guard she did fulfil –
chipped at the hall as the sun rose in the sky:
'Die, lady of the night! Die, monster, die!'

Services rendered, home the lord came riding;
On his return, they brought him grievous tidings:
'Master, your son – your little lad is dead,
 as for your wife – the lily hangs its head!'

"Oh, mother, mother, an evil snake are you!
What kind of harm did my wife ever do?
As you have poisoned my life's sweetest flower,
May God's world blacken for you in this hour!"

The Daughter's Curse

"Why do you look so sad and tearful,
                              Daughter mine?
Why do you look so sad and tearful?
You used to be so gay and cheerful –
    Where did all your laughter go?"

'I have killed a little dove,
                              Mother mine;
I have killed a little dove,
Left all lonely and unloved –
    And it was as white as snow!'

"That was no dove – you look so strange,
                              Daughter mine!
That was no dove – you look so strange,
With your pretty face quite changed –
    Wracked and wrenched you look to me!"

'A tiny baby I have slain,
                              Mother mine!
A tiny baby I have slain,
My own poor child, new-born in pain –
    Now I could die of misery!'

"And what do you intend to do,
                    Daughter mine?
And what do you intend to do
To lift the guilt that weighs on you,
    And reconcile God's angry will?"

'Oh, I shall go to seek that flower,
                    Mother mine!
Oh, I shall go to seek that flower,
Which to cleanse guilt has sovereign power,
    And troubled blood can cool and still.'

"Tell me, where may that flower be found,
                    Daughter mine?
Tell me, where may that flower be found,
In all the wide world's endless round?
    In what garden does it grow?"

'There on that mound beside the gate,
                    Mother mine!
There on that mound beside the gate,
On a nail in that pillar driven straight,
    And on the hempen rope below.'

"And what will you bequeath that boy,
                    Daughter mine?
And what will you bequeath that boy,
Who visited our house with joy,
    And with you found his happiness?"

'To him a blessing I will send,
                    Mother mine!
To him a blessing I will send –
A worm in his soul till his life's end,
    For all his words of faithlessness!'

"And what gift will you leave your mother,
                    Daughter mine?
And what gift will you leave your mother,
She who loved you like no other,
    And cared for you so tenderly?"

'My curse to you I leave behind,
                    Mother mine!
My curse to you I leave behind –
That in the grave no peace you'll find,
    For the wilful heart you gave to me!'

The Prophetess

Whenever to your eye a tear is springing,
    And heavy times fall to your share,
A sprig of hope to you I shall be bringing,
    Prophecies shall my voice declare.

The spirit of prophecy comes from on high –
    Do not weigh lightly what I say;
Necessity's law on the whole world does lie,
    And every man his debt must pay.

The river seeks its end in the ocean's main;
    The flame leaps up towards the skies;
What Earth creates, she herself destroys again,
    Nothing in vain, though, lives and dies.

Certain and steady are the footsteps of fate;
    What has to happen, comes about;
And what one day conceals in its torrents' spate
    The next once more to the world brings out.

* * *

A man I saw, by Bělin's waters flowing,
    The ancestor of dukes so great,
Behind his plough through the village he was going,
    The fruits of the earth to cultivate.
From the meeting men came, and as prince addressed him –

    The ploughman they had been sent to find –
In garments all shining with gold they dressed him;
    The half-ploughed field he left behind.

He laid down his plough, freed the oxen of their load:
    'Wherever you came from, back you go!'
and there in the field he planted his goad,
    so that leaf and blossom from it did grow.

The oxen were swallowed by a hill near by –
    Foul waters mark it to our days;
And the naked bark of the hazel-branch dry
    Sprouted three strong and healthy sprays.

The rods bore blossom and fruit, all three,
    But one alone matured to thrive;
The other two withered and fell from the tree –
    To this day, they have not revived.

Listen and know – these words are not in vain!
    Commit them carefully to mind:
The age returns, the times come again,
    When even dead twigs new life will find.

Both of those branches with their noble flower
    Far and wide with new strength will shoot,
To the world's surprise, in an unforeseen hour,
    Bearing a crop of blessed fruit.

Then a prince, all clad in purple and gold,

Will come the ancient debt to pay;
Přemysl's cast-off plough from the dust and mould
    He'll bring back to the light of day.

The oxen he will call from the hollow hill,
    And yoke them to the plough again;
The long-neglected field to the end he'll till,
    Scattering it with golden grain.

And that seed will sprout, and the spring-wheat will thrive;
    Bright will shine golden ears of corn;
The country's fortunes with them will come alive,
    And ancient glory be reborn.

* * *

Over the river I saw a rock looming –
    On the rocky bluff Krok's golden towers;
All around the castle, meadows were blooming –
    Princess Libuše's garden of flowers.

Below the castle there stands a charming place –
    The riverside baths of our princess;
There I saw the lady with her noble face –
    Shining with silver was her dress.

Standing on the threshold of her baths so dear,
    Watching the river's troubled spate,
She read out this judgment, words of hope and fear:
    Her much-loved country's secret fate.

'I see bloody wars and conflagration,
    a sharp sword piercing you to the bone,
I see your sorrow, your humiliation:
    Do not lose hope, my folk, my own!'

There came two maidens, standing at her side;
    A golden cradle to her they gave;
She kissed it, and then, in the bottomless tide
    Sank it below the cliff in the waves.

Listen, and know all the words Libuše said –
    I myself heard what she foresaw:
'Rest for a while in this place, my own son's bed,
    till I shall summon you once more!

A youthful new world will arise at that time
    Out of the ocean deep's dark womb;
In my fathers' courtyard the broad-branching limes
    Fragrantly once again will bloom.

A gloomy harvest revives with heavy showers;
    A radiant day is born from night:
And the race which long ago knew glorious hours
    Once more will shine with glory bright.

Forth to the light, from the river's chasm great,
    The golden cradle will float by;
The land's salvation, for ages marked by fate,
    There at rest as a babe shall lie.'

* * *

Blessed, holy bed, I have seen you before –
   You, my star, I know already!
But until the time I behold you once more,
   Rest assured, stay calm and steady.

Summer after summer ceaselessly hastens;
   And winter chasing winter goes:
But my confident trust still abides unshaken,
   And like the year, my firm hope grows.

When in summer, from deep pools beneath the rock
   Every single youth shall come back,
And when in the winter, in a merry flock,
   The ice beneath their sleds shall crack,

'See where for Libuše's army,' I shall sigh,
   'many new members once more grow!
When will come the age, when at rest I may lie?
   That time is not yet here – ah, no!'

For in the books of fate it stands in writing:
   Listen and know what I foretell;
'The dead, when that blessed dawn the sky is lighting,
   in its honour shall rise as well.

And Libuše then, with all that mighty band,
   Leading her troops will take her place;
And stretching from on high her motherly hand,
   Bring glory to her own Czech race!'

* * *

By the Orlice river a church I saw,
    Of its golden bell I heard the chime,
Before violent passions' turbulence tore
    The simple Czech heart of ancient times.

When faith, hope and charity no more were found –
    God's virtues – in Bohemia's land,
The church disappeared in earth's depths underground;
    Waters washed where it used to stand.

But not for ever in its grave will it stay:
    Once again will the waters fall,
And the church rise up in its former array;
    Gloriously will the bell's voice call.

Listen and know what in writing stands enrolled,
    And lies in fate established well:
'The dawn of a golden age you shall behold,
    Awakened by the golden bell.'

By the Orlice river, there on the hill,
    The wind will sow a forest new,
The young wood mature in its time, until
    Those full-grown firs shall flourish too;

And the last surviving fir of all that wood
    Shall in due time live out its day,
Wither, and fall dead into Orlice's flood;
    Even the root shall then decay.

And then, hunted through, there shall come a wild sow
    And dig the last fragments with her snout:
From the ruins and rubble beneath them now
    The golden bell once more shines out.

For thus from the earliest age it was ordained:
    That it should journey underground,
And in its time to the goal to which it strained,
    Over the river, a way be found.'

Know that on the hillside, under fir-trees green,
    Fate's chosen trunk already grows:
Lofty and mighty, scarce a branch to be seen,
    Only a fresh new crown it shows.

Is the bell, too, moving to its destination?
    Will it, in time, attain its end?
Who can give true and certain information?
    Who a message of hope can send?

Ah, I saw in a field near Bystřice how
    A peasant sang in humility
His morning hymn as he walked behind his plough:
    'O God, o holy Trinity!'

Then a curious obstacle fouled his plough –
    Shaft from fork was pulled with a wrench:
'What devil from hell froze that up for me now?
    May both of them fall down through the trench!'

Thus cursed the ploughman, and down there came, falling
    Into the hollow, the deep-voiced chime
Of the golden bell, so plaintively calling,
    'Ah, not yet, this is not the time!'

Ah, not yet – for the time is not yet here!
    Incline your ear, though, to the ground,
And underneath the fir-trees' roots you will hear
    The golden bell's far-distant sound.

* * *

Do not lament that calamity and fate
    Struck you many a heavy blow;
Rather lament that to face them, to this date,
    Greater wisdom you did not show!

I see a mountain over others towering –
    A mountain famed throughout your lands –
Circled with gardens vigorously flowering,
    And on that mountain God's church stands.

But to the church three gates the way are leading,
    And three go out of it, still apart;
Hear and know what is written for your reading,
    And take this prophecy to heart:

'The flame of hope you are nourishing in vain!
    Your grief and hardship will know no term,
Until they walk through a single gate again,
    Bohemia's folk will not stand firm!'

You to whom the gift of ears to hear was given,
    Why with thumbs do you block them shut?
And you to whom reason came down from heaven,
    Why do you tread it underfoot?

Since Svatopluk taught his dear sons to agree,
    A thousand years have vanished hence;
But there has not pierced to this hour, I can see,
    The golden sound of words of sense!

* * *

You who, knowing your fathers' glorious actions,
    Gladly boast of them in your pride,
Look in Prague by a pillar, where a fraction
    Of a hero stands on the bridge's side.

The head has crumbled; rains have washed it away,
    And the Swedish war destroyed the breast;
But the belly and legs stand fast to this day,
    And the foolish trappings of pride still rest.

Say not in vain, 'Those are relics of the old times,
    Toppling stones, all cracked and broken!'
Know that for the heroes of your own times
    These provide a fateful token.

Listen to my words, and note them all with care:
    Do not trouble to hope in vain,
Till an ardent heart above that belly there
    And a right true head shall grow again!

MORE INFORMATION ON
THE AMBER POETS SERIES

In November 2013, Jantar published its third title, *Kytice*, in a bi-lingual edition in a print-on-demand, paperback format that was available to purchase world-wide via various online book outlets. We also printed 50 copies for ourselves to sell at a launch event at UCL School of Slavonic and East European Studies in London. Another 50 copies were printed for the Shakespeare and Sons bookshop in Prague.

Buried somewhere in many people's photo files are photos of that event. Wine and beer was involved and possibly some crisps. Susan Reynolds, who translated this volume, would have baked a batch of her famous cheese straws and they were probably snapped up very quickly. What remains in my memory is that all enjoyed a splendid evening. All 50 copies were sold at the event; and I regretted sending the other 50 copies to the Shakespeare and Sons bookshop in Prague.

I had advised the editor of the Czech-language newsletter, *Britské Listy*, of *Kytice*'s publication date and the following morning, readers began queueing outside the Shakespeare and Sons bookshop in Prague before the proprietor arrived to open up. He was quite surprised to see so many people outside his shop before it opened and even more surprised when he was told why. He had bad news for them, the books hadn't arrived. However, he did make a note of names and numbers and promised to call when copies of *Kytice* were delivered. More and more readers popped into the shop asking for the book over the following days and weeks and more copies were ordered from Jantar HQ in London. More copies were printed and sent to them.

In February 2014, a very positive review of *Kytice* was published in *The Times Literary Supplement*, written by Zuzana Slobodová. (This was the first ever review to appear featuring a Jantar title). Then in March, *The New York Times* published an interview with the novelist, Helen Oyeyemi, in its regular *By The Book* column. In that piece, Helen described *Kytice* as her favourite book. (Quotes from both reviews are on the back cover of this edition). Then in April, Jantar HQ began receiving emails from many readers asking why *Kytice* was 43 in the Poetry Bestseller listings on Amazon.com. We had no idea, though we did check the listing and discovered that *Kytice* had jumped to 41. *Kytice* remained in those listings till early May, by which time, we had discovered the interview with Helen Oyeyemi online. In May 2014, Jantar printed a hardback version of *Kytice* for sale in the Czech Republic to coincide with Susan Reynolds's visit to the Svět Knihy Bookfair in Prague. Susan was only in Prague for a few days but squeezed in two live interviews broadcast on Czech TV and at least four public readings. (There may have been more).

In late 2019, I met the Czech artist, Míla Fürstová at an event at the Czech Ambassador's Residence in Hampstead, London. We spoke for at least two hours about a wide range of topics including the poems in *Kytice*. The poems were read to her by her grandmother when she was a child and she had produced a piece of art that had been used in the opening titles of a Czech crime drama called *Vodník [The Water-goblin]*. (The opening title sequence was on YouTube somewhere if I cared to look for them. I did).

A few months before I met Míla, most of remaining copies of *Kytice* were destroyed in fire where they were stored just outside Prague. (The surviving copies still smell of smoke!).

I had been seeking something special to celebrate the 10th anniversary of Jantar's foundation in 2021 and asked Míla if she would consider creating a cover for a new edition. She said she would think about it and I promised I would send her a copy of the poems. Things moved rapidly after that. Czech Publisher, Euromedia Group, had recently published a handsome volume of her art including some used for the cover of Coldplay's *Ghost Stories* CD and some single releases. It was suggested by the Czech publisher that Jantar enter a joint venture to produce an illustrated edition of *Kytice*. A few months later, the COVID pandemic struck and during that awful time, Míla kept herself busy (and distracted) producing 10 etchings based on 10 of the poems in *Kytice*. The whole process was a very welcome escape from all the horror of COVID.

Euromedia Group published new illustrated Czech versions of *Kytice* featuring this artwork in separate imprints, Odeón and Knižní Klub, in November 2019. Jantar produced an English-only edition featuring the same artwork with a new introduction by the musicologist Geoffrey Chew along with some fragments of other poems written by Karel Jaromír Erben in November 2020. During the editing phase, it was discovered that 2020 was the 150th anniversary of Erben's death, so it was decided to bring forward the publication date for what was to become the second edition to Christmas 2020. (In the end, Jantar's 10th anniversary in March 2021 went largely unnoticed as most of the world was in lockdown at time. Jantar posted a handwritten note on 31 March on its social media assets). The major poems (but not the fragments) and the introduction by Professor Chew are reproduced in this volume.

Jantar was hacked in 2017 and much data, draft manuscripts, sales and financial records were lost. In the second week of lockdown, Bertrams, our UK distributor, who had previously been enthusiastically marketing our books went into voluntary liquidation. Brexit closed our largest and most profitable sales channel: direct sales to readers in the EU. The fire destroying the last unsold copies of the original version of *Kytice* has already been mentioned. Cuts to funding arts programmes, huge increases in the cost of printing and distribution, reduced space devoted to book reviews in print and online media outlets have not made publishing easy.

So why start publishing poetry now?! The answer is that there are many, many outstanding poetry collections that remain untranslated into English and many readers who want to read them. Another truth is that we had been contemplating publishing poetry since 2011 when the company was founded. We knew that there was a strong interested in poetry translated into English. However, simply keeping Jantar going was a tough gig, expanding its offering was simply judged too tough and we carried on with the prose.

In 2023, Jantar was approached by Helen Vassallo, an academic at Exter University. She had reviewed a Jantar title on her ground-breaking *Women in Translation* blog a few years earlier. It is fair to say that we respect her as an academic, cultural activist and awesome human being. Helen asked if we would consider publishing a collection of poems written by the Ukrainian soldier-poet, Artur Dron'. The sample translations of those poems were outstanding and we said yes very quickly. The conceit and design of what became THE AMBER POETS series also took shape very quickly because it had been mulled upon for a very long time. The cover design concept was inspired by Faber's paperback cover artwork from the 1970s and 1980s. The series title, THE AMBER POETS, was inspired by Penguin's European Poets series, again from the 1970s and 1980s. It was thought that the Amber Poets was a little bit arrogant, possibly dillusional. However, the name does align neatly with Jantar, which means Amber, and if anything can be trapped in amber, well, poetry published in languages other than English is exactly that. So, we are suddenly at the moment when Artur's collection, *We Were Here*, was published nearly a year ago. (Artur's frontline unit was attacked by a Russian drone on the week of publication. Two of Artur's comrades were killed. Artur's left arm was badly wounded by shrapnel. He is still recovering). Volume 2 of the Amber Poets is our third edition of *Kytice*, the first actual collection of poems we published in 2013. Amber Poets Volume 3 is *[dasein: defence of presence]* by Ukrainain activist, translator, poet and soldier, Yaryna Chornohuz. Further volumes by Nicolau Dols, Renée Vivien, Hviezdoslav and others are being prepared for publication next year and beyond. The interest in this series has been much higher than expected and all the more heart-warming for that. It is a huge and happy thing.

Thank you for reading this far.

Keep well and keep reading!

Michael Tate
Publisher

PS. There is much more information on our little publisher online generally but specifically on
www.JantarPublishing.com